"President" Trump's America

Earl Ofari Hutchinson

Middle Passage Press
Los Angeles, CA

Publisher's Cataloging-in-Publication Data

Names: Hutchinson, Earl Ofari.
Title: "President" Trump's America / Earl Ofari Hutchinson.
Description: Los Angeles, CA : Middle Passage Press, 2024. | Includes
   bibliographic references and index.
Identifiers: LCCN 2024913211 | ISBN 9798894801056 (pbk.)
Subjects: LCSH: Trump, Donald, 1946- . | Trump, Donald, 1946- – Political
   and social views. | Presidents – United States – Election – 2024. | United
   States – Politics and government – 2017-2021. | United States – Politics and
   government – 2021- . | BISAC: POLITICAL SCIENCE / American Government
   / Executive Branch. | POLITICAL SCIENCE / Political Process / Campaigns &
   Elections. | POLITICAL SCIENCE / Public Policy / General.
Classification: LCC E912 H88 2024 | DDC 973.933 H--dc23
LC record available at https://lccn.loc.gov/2024913211

Table of Contents

Introduction

Former President Donald Trump, as of May 2024, was a convicted felon. But that in no way seemed to take away from his shocking off-the-cuff quip that he wanted to be a dictator. That drew much chatter, puzzlement, and anger when he made it in December 2023 in an interview with a *New York Times* writer. Whether a convicted felon or not, the thought of being a dictator was then, and possibly after the conviction, still probably very much on his mind.

When he had the chance to walk the quip back, he really didn't. During a speech to the New York Young Republican Club the same month, he claimed, "I didn't say that. I said I want to be a dictator for one day. You know why I wanted to be a dictator? Because I want a wall, and I want to drill, drill, drill."

It was not much of a retraction. In fact, one might surmise that Trump's rule as a dictator was very much in his thinking. It was the third time that he referenced his dictator fantasy. The other was during an event with *Fox News* host Sean Hannity.

Then he supposedly made light of it by saying that after he gave *carte blanche* to the oil and gas conglomerates to drill to their hearts' content with no checks and clamped down the border, then he'd hand in his dictatorship. As he put it, "After that, I'm not a dictator, OK?"

The dictator quip and the momentary furor it sparked was another Trump media sideshow. What was not a sideshow was the context in which he tossed out the dictator bit. He explicitly cited the bitterly divisive issues of immigration and drilling. Trump during the 2024 presidential campaign repeatedly made both his signature issues.

The shocking and sudden exit from the race in July 2024 of President Joe Biden, until then Trump's whipping post rival, didn't change anything. He continued the assault on his Biden-replacement opponent, Vice President Kamala Harris, on these issues.

However, immigration and unregulated drilling were not by any stretch the only issues that he made outsized promises to tackle at campaign rallies, in interviews, in posts on his social media outlets, and most importantly, in a big, wordy, but detailed agenda labeled *Agenda 47*—the number 47 being the number of Trump's hoped-for second presidency.

In this document, he laid out a sweeping plan for a second four-year reign in the Oval Office to radically change government policy on education, jobs, health, gender and racial equity, China relations, the military, and foreign policy, as well as energy and immigration policy. Trump wrapped himself tightly in the garb of nobility as one who was on a near divine mission to save America: "I left behind my former life because I could not sit by and watch career politicians continue bleeding this country dry and allow other nations to take advantage of us on trade, borders, foreign policy, and national defense."

Political analyst Earl Ofari Hutchinson, in his forthcoming book *"President" Trump's America* (Middle Passage Press), details the specifics of *Agenda 47*. He assesses the impact of the major Trump issues—the role of the federal government, education, immigration, energy policy, the military, the use and misuse of executive orders, ethnic and gender diversity, handling of the economy, gun control, the impact of the assassination attempt on him, and an aggressive trade and tariff war with China. He examines the truth and falsity in Trump's relationship with *Project 2025*. He tells exactly how the Trump agenda will spark a titanic fight that would plunge the country into endless debate, turmoil, and division.

He further tells how and why Trump's vision of America and his vow to shatter "The Deep State" would be the greatest transformation of American society since the nation's founding. *"President" Trump's America* presents a riveting answer to the question: Was Trump really joking about being a dictator?

1

"Send Them All Back"

"Far more illegal immigrants have entered the United States in the last two years than at any time in American history, and by a massive margin. We've never seen anything like it. Our country is under invasion."
—Trump, from *Agenda 47*

As expected, the rapturous crowd in Dubuque, Iowa went wild in September 2023 when Trump shouted that if he were re-elected, he'd conduct "the largest domestic deportation operation in American history." This was not just campaign hyperbole.

Trump had practically made it his sacred mantra before, during, and after the 2016 presidential election that he would implement an iron-fisted clampdown on illegal immigration. He repeatedly bragged that he had turned off the illegal immigration faucet when he was president, claiming that the nation had the securest border it had ever had. He first shouted this claim during the 2024 presidential campaign at a rally in New Hampshire in January 2023, saying "28,000 soldiers guarding our border and we had the best border numbers that we ever have. We had the safest border in the history of our country and all Biden had to do was go to the beach and relax... But he would go to the beach and say let's dismantle."

At nearly every campaign stop afterward the crowd heard him spout this claim or some variation of it. There was certainly much to dispute about that claim.

*****

Trump's grandiose deportation promise was not a reminder of the past but a policy initiative that would have sweeping implications for American society in the future—if he was back in the Oval Office. He ticked off exactly how he'd cleanse the country of illegal immigrants.

He'd wipe off the books Biden's executive order that liberalized the asylum process. He'd finish building his oft promised border wall. He'd invoke the Alien Enemies Act to purge the nation of gang members, drug dealers, and cartel members supposedly pouring into the U.S.

He'd flood the border with troops, FBI agents, the DEA, Homeland Security, the Bureau of Alcohol, Tobacco, Firearms and Explosives (ATF) agents, and U.S. special forces. Their job would be to stop what he branded "the invasion" of the nation by illegals.

If that weren't enough, he'd deploy the U.S. Navy to blockade the coast and board ships suspected of harboring drug-dealing illegals. He'd ship the children sent here during the Obama and Biden years in office out of humanitarian concern right back to the countries they came from.

He'd reimpose his other signature and highly contentious and controversial initiative—the Muslim travel ban. He imposed that in 2017 and spent the next year in pitched battles with Democrats, civil liberty groups, and the courts over the ban. No matter; he'd bring it back again.

*****

Trump fully intended to take the war on illegal immigration to new, terrifying heights no matter the dubious legality, fallout, and certain negative consequences. There would be many.

The first would be to again roil the administration in a never-ending round of pitched court battles, lawsuits, and legal action. Another would be to skirt if not violate the legal tenets of the nation's long-standing established immigration laws and policies—those would be challenged at every turn.

Another fallout would be the drastic revision of the use of government enforcement agencies and federal law enforcement personnel. He would pull hundreds if not thousands of agents from their other duties solely to police immigration enforcement.

Yet another consequence would be his plan to pour massive amounts of federal dollars into implementing the crackdown. That was money that would have to be pulled from the federal budget allocated for the broad range of federal law enforcement duties.

The greatest worry and danger was the effect this would have on the nation's economy. This was not mere speculation. The numbers backed up the worry. In 2023, the Congressional Budget Office reported that the U.S. labor force would grow by 5.2 million people by 2033.

The growth would be due almost exclusively to net immigration. The surge in the workforce translated out to hard dollars for the economy to the tune of seven trillion dollars more than it would have grown without new immigrants.

The unstated damage was that without that workforce rise from immigration, unemployment would jump and there would be a big downturn in economic growth. "The economy is not a zero-sum game," said Chloe East, an economist at the University of Colorado, Denver who focuses on immigration policy. "When one person has a job, which does not mean one less job for somebody else. We can say for sure that would translate into a higher unemployment rate for U.S.-born workers. That is not a temporary effect."

Other experts on the economic upside of illegal immigration to the nation made a similar point. "The work of the U.S. citizen serving a table in a restaurant is complemented by the work of a possibly unauthorized worker in the back of the restaurant," noted Michael Clemens, an economist specializing in international migration at George Mason University. "Neither of those jobs can happen without the other."

Then there was the impact on the construction industry. Like restaurants and other service industries, the construction industry relies heavily on undocumented labor. One labor expert noted that "it would be quite daunting" for everyone attached to the housing and construction market "if we were to vacate 11 million people from our population. We would see rising costs in housing, especially here in Dallas, where we see a lot of labor from immigrants. I just see that as being a natural consequence. A devastating effect."

*****

The standard counter from Trump and the America First "eradicate illegal immigration" crowd was twofold. One was that illegal immigrants drag down wages.

The other was that low-income, unskilled workers, especially Black and Hispanic workers, are virtually shoved out of the job market by illegal immigrants. These concerns touched a nerve among many Black, Hispanic, and low wage workers. In fact, some research did bear out they had reason for concern. However, other research countered that the lower wages brought greater profit for employers. Presumably, the gains from immigration—both legal and illegal—would grow the economy and therefore benefit American-born workers at all levels.

*****

In his first term, Trump signed dozens of executive orders on immigration that stretched far beyond the seemingly narrow confine of the issue. In a talk to Department of Homeland Security employees in April 2017, he laid down his get-tough gauntlet on illegal immigration, saying "Beginning today, the United States of America gets back control of its borders."

He then signed two of the executive orders that set the template for the crackdown. The first was Trump's much ballyhooed and much reviled border wall. He ordered Homeland Security to plan, design, and find the money for the wall.

The interesting side note on this was that with much fanfare Trump repeatedly claimed that he squeezed enough money out to build more than one hundred new miles of what he boastfully characterized as a "long, tall and very powerful" border wall. It was true that by the end of his term more than one hundred miles of wall were added to the border.

The one inconvenient fact that Trump failed to add was that most of the miles of the wall were not new. They were simply a repair and replacement of the barrier that was already in place. Trump's math, then, was slightly off. The correct figure of the amount of new wall built was exactly one, not more than one, mile of actual new wall built where there was no previous barrier. Yet Trump still got his DHS officials to back him up on his claim that he got a big part of his much-demanded border wall built.

The other major component of the executive order was Trump's pledge to massively flood the border with thousands of more border patrol agents and immigration officials. Their task would be to interrogate, detain, search, and most importantly arrest all non-citizens or non-nationals.

Once they were arrested, they'd be jailed in the massively expanded number of detention centers Trump demanded to be built at the border. Once they were nabbed and detained, if they had been convicted or were suspected of engaging in any criminal actions, which according to the order could be anyone an immigration official felt endangered "public safety or national security," they'd be speedily deported.

To ensure that no illegal immigrant charged with a crime slipped through the net, it mandated that all local law enforcement agencies in cities hand over the illegal immigrants' fingerprints and any arrest data to immigration officials to enable them to track down illegal immigrants in the country who had committed crimes.

The order would virtually put an end to another Obama and Biden administrations' policy that was hotly disputed by conservatives. That was the examination on a case-by-case basis of the status of illegal immigrants to determine whether they should be allowed to remain in the country based on humanitarian considerations.

Trump also took dead aim at sanctuary cities in his executive orders. The message to those cities that declared themselves an arrest-free haven for illegal immigrants was that they wouldn't get a penny of federal grant money until they dropped their sanctuary designation.

Trump took one added step that had never been a part of any immigration law provision. He ordered the U.S. Immigration and Customs Enforcement to establish an Office for Victims of Crimes Committed by Removable Aliens. The unwieldy Orwellian-sounding named office would issue quarterly reports on the harm that alleged crime-prone illegal immigrants did to victims and, by extension, to the country. Said Trump on this in his talk to Homeland Security employees on signing the orders:

"I have no higher duty than to protect the lives of the American people. First, these families lost their loved ones, then they endured a system that ignore them, while at the same time constantly rewarding those who broke the law."

*****

The orders Trump signed during his term impacted just about all areas of federal authority. It laid a firm foundation as well for a radical overhaul of immigration law and policy in American life. The impact would be on law enforcement, the courts, state and local judiciary, labor, the economy, travel, transportation, human rights, civil liberties, education, health care, crime and violence, and ethnic and racial stereotypes.

Trump's sweeping radical immigration overhaul dictate was roundly attacked and challenged every step of the way by Democrats, civil rights and civil liberties groups, and immigration reform groups. They opposed it in Congress, state legislatures, and the courts. The opponents won a number of significant victories that stymied the full implementation of the Trumpian measures.

However, Trump had laid a firm template for escalating on an even more massive scale the assault on illegal immigration if he got the chance in a second term. In a second go-round, he'd have another advantage. That was public concern, even anger, over illegal immigration.

Polls during the 2024 presidential campaign repeatedly found that immigration ranked at or near the top of public worry. A solid majority of Americans wanted tougher action to stem the flow of illegal immigrants into the country.

Trump banked that his tough talk and presumed tougher action was exactly the action that the public wanted and could be his ticket back to the White House. He intended to again milk the issue for all it was worth.

2

"I Am the Law-and-Order President"

"Joe Biden and the 'Defund the Police' Democrats have turned our once great cities into cesspools of bloodshed and crime."
—Trump, from *Agenda 47*

In his 2016 winning presidential campaign and again in his 2020 losing presidential campaign, Trump loudly declared himself the "law-and-order candidate." That wasn't good enough. He soon branded himself the "President of law and order."

Even that wasn't good enough. Following the raucous, ballooning protests over police violence after the police slaying of George Floyd in May 2020, Trump tweeted in big, bold letters "LAW & ORDER." His multi-count conviction in May 2024 and his official designation as a convicted felon didn't faze him. He didn't back away one inch from the self-imposed label of the law-and-order president that he had slapped on himself.

His self-designation as Mr. Law and Order was an unabashed, uncredited lift from the 1968 presidential campaign playbook of then GOP presidential candidate Richard Nixon. Nixon, less loudly but just as pointedly, declared that he'd be the law-and-order president whose administration would wage relentless war against crime in the streets and against permissiveness.

Trump changed only one thing from the Nixon copycat script for his 2024 presidential campaign. He added more body to the story line. He'd spend billions more to hire, retain, and train hordes of new police. He'd demand that as a price for police departments to get DOJ funding they'd have to aggressively employ stop and frisk searches, crack down on all drug users, immediately deport all alleged crime-prone aliens, and bust up all criminal cartel gangs.

He'd totally overhaul the DOJ, at the total expense of scrapping civil rights enforcement, to focus solely on nabbing violent criminals. He'd send in the National Guard to any city that Democrats supposedly had turned into lawless havens. He'd be a vigorous defender and protector of open carry gun-toting and "stand your ground" laws.

He ended all this with a ringing declaration to take back America's streets from the lawless of all stripes. All of this would, he crowed, Make America Safe Again.

*****

There was not a word in his law-and-order to-do list about defending civil rights, civil liberties, or upholding constitutional protections. There was not a word about the courts and local prosecutors' role in trials and prosecutions. There was not a word about the prosecution of racial, gender, religious, and same-sex hate-motivated crimes.

There was not a word about investigating and prosecuting police misconduct, abuse, or the overuse of deadly force. In Trump's take-back-the-streets America, the word "reform" was tantamount to a dirty word. He didn't deem it worthy of even a faint mention.

The one exception came at the tail end of his first term. He ripped those critics who lambasted him for his lack of any nod to civil rights protections: "In recent days, there has been vigorous discussion about how to ensure fairness, equality, and justice for all of our people. Unfortunately, there's some trying to stoke division and to push an extreme agenda—which we won't go for—that will produce only more poverty, more crime, more suffering. This includes radical efforts to defund, dismantle, and disband the police."

Trump's ratcheted-up tough talk on crime for a second term didn't mean merely passing and enforcing tougher laws on the big-ticket crimes such as murder, arson, rape, armed robbery, carjackings, and assorted other violent acts. Those were crimes in which the offenders cut across all ethnic, religious, and gender lines. Yet in Trump's law and order plan, the perpetrators were almost exclusively Blacks and Hispanics.

He repeatedly touted his law-and-order line in railing at protests over the police killing of George Floyd. His special target was Black Lives Matter supporters. He repeatedly blasted the mild violence that occurred after a handful of protests. At the same time, he virtually gave a pass to the neo-Nazi marchers who did commit major acts of violence, including murder, at several of their marches.

There were two near textbook examples of just who Trump's calculated, race-baiting, law-and-order pitch was aimed at. Following a neo-Nazi and KKK members march in Charlottesville, Virginia, in 2017, in which one of them murdered a counter-protester, Trump labeled them among the "very fine people on both sides."

The other example: Trump gave a back door nod to Kyle Rittenhouse, the seventeen-year-old Neo-Nazi-influenced vigilante who murdered two people at a Black Lives Matter protest in Kenosha, Wisconsin in August 2020: "He was trying to get away from them, I guess, it looks like, and he fell, and then they very violently attacked him."

When Rittenhouse was acquitted in November 2021, Trump had plenty to say: "Congratulations to Kyle Rittenhouse for being found INNOCENT of all charges." He didn't stop there with his gush over him, saying "It's called being found NOT GUILTY—And by the way, if that's not self-defense, nothing is!"

This was an easy call for Trump to make in backing the Neo-Nazis and Rittenhouse's murderous act. Both fit the Trump narrative that violent crime comes almost exclusively with a Black or Hispanic face, and that draconian punishment was the antidote.

The big pay-off though was something that presidents Nixon, Clinton, Reagan, and Bush Sr. knew and exploited— that "law and order," "crime in the streets," and "jail 'em fast and often" were always political game winners with many Americans.

"All of this rhetoric about invasion, rioting, and crime is part of a broader appeal to fear, an emotion to which conservatives have historically responded," said Ted Johnson, a senior fellow at the Brennan Center for Justice. "That is a scare tactic used to incite people's fears and anxieties against others."

Trump and the GOP, starting first with GOP presidential candidate Barry Goldwater in 1964 and refined by Nixon in 1968, have been masters at employing this proven vote-getting scare tact. However, it bears repeating that Democrats Clinton, and to a lesser extent former President Obama, also felt the pressure from the law-and-order right, so at times burnished their credentials as tough on crime advocates.

*****

In a second term, Trump would zero in on other areas of the criminal justice system to ensure that the harshest punishments would be meted out to his targets. He would appoint even more young, hardline conservative judges to the federal judiciary during his term.

They would be unhesitating in imposing the toughest sentences on defendants. Trump would aggressively assail and undermine the efforts in states that have implemented significant criminal justice reform initiatives, such as the reduction or elimination of the bail requirement for low income, impoverished, mostly minorities who were accused of low level, petty, non-violent crime. With high bail requirements reinstated, those defendants would languish behind bars for even longer stretches of time.

There would be two other far-reaching consequences of a Trump police run, empowering America in reversing the modest criminal justice reform efforts at the state and federal level. One major example was the George Floyd Justice in Policing Act of 2021 passed by the House in March 2021. It was killed in the Senate. That bill would be a dead relic of the past during a Trump second term.

The other is that many states would conceivably take the cue and reinstitute such measures as three strikes laws, more stringent probation and parole requirements, a reduction in the number of clemency and pardon grants, and the curtailment of house confinement, monitoring, and community service in lieu of jailing.

This was not speculation. Many states and cities didn't wait for Trump's possible re-election to swing into their tough on crime action. They weren't all state GOP-controlled state legislatures, governorships, and citizens groups either. In 2023 voters in liberal, Democratic top-heavy San Francisco passed two initiatives that gave more power to police and that mandated drug treatment in order to receive welfare. More than a million people signed on to qualify a tough-on-crime initiative on the November 2024 ballot in blue state California.

It was no surprise that red states such as Louisiana, Wyoming, Iowa, Oklahoma, Texas, and Tennessee, to name a few, beat back all attempts at various criminal justice reform measures. In almost all cases, the measures were proposed by Democrats in the legislatures, legislatures in which they were the minority.

The consequence of the reform measures passed during the Obama administration and by Democratic-controlled state legislatures was a sharp reduction in incarceration in the U.S. The nation, though, still retained its ranking as the world's number one incarcerator. However, with the trend toward criminal justice reform reversal and the colossal push it would get from Trump, the U.S. would almost certainly top its own record in the number of persons behind federal and state prison bars, the majority of whom would continue to be poor, Black, and Hispanic. Most of them again would not be there for crimes such as murder or rape, but for nonviolent, petty and drug-use related crimes.

Law and order would no longer be a cheap pandering, emotion stirring, fear and hysteria ploy. Nor would it simply be a racist wink and nod dog whistle. It would be resurrected and then codified as the new norm in American criminal law enforcement. Trump's assault on criminal justice reforms would usher in a full-blown quasi police state, with civil liberties trashed, minimal civilian or legislative accountability, transparency, watchdog, or oversight roles.

The ultimate irony was that Trump's law and order America would be wildly at odds with the man who himself was a convicted felon. But then again, the other President, namely Nixon, who popularized the law-and-order pitch and whom Trump shamelessly pilfered it from, himself was caught red-handed in criminal action that subsequently resulted in his resignation from the presidency. History indeed under a second Trump term would frightenedly repeat itself.

3

Taking Back the Schools

"Our secret weapon will be the college accreditation system. It's called accreditation for a reason.

The accreditors are supposed to ensure that schools are not ripping off students and taxpayers, but they have failed totally. When I return to the White House, I will fire the radical Left accreditors that have allowed our colleges to become dominated by Marxist Maniacs and lunatics.

These standards will include defending the American tradition and Western civilization, protecting free speech, eliminating wasteful administrative positions that drive up costs incredibly, removing all Marxist diversity, equity, and inclusion bureaucrats."

—Trump, from *Agenda 47*

Trump could not have been more emphatic in his campaign video in September 2023, announcing what he had in store for America's education system if and when he returned to the Oval Office. "We're going to end education coming out of Washington, D.C. We're going to close it up—all those buildings all over the place and people that in many cases hate our children. We're going to send it all back to the states."

He then dropped the punch line: he'd immediately get rid of the Department of Education. The tip-off about just who this was designed to appeal to was in the declaration that "they" hate our children.

In a lengthy talk at the Conservative Political Action Conference in 2023, Trump left no doubt about what he really meant by that and what it meant for the nation's schools: "Across the country, we need to implement strict prohibitions on teaching inappropriate racial, sexual, and political material to America's schoolchildren in any form whatsoever. And if federal bureaucrats are going to push this radicalism, we should abolish the Department of Education."

Trump's planned assault on education had little to do with improving the quality, standards, or level and type of education of students of all genders and ethnicities. It was another naked political harangue of his and the ultra-conservatives' favorite whipping boys, the so-called "Radical Marxist" DEI and liberal education reform advocates.

*****

It was more than emotional political pandering to Trump's base. There was a carefully honed detailed plan to implement it.

Trump would rigorously investigate and then end any funding for schools that allegedly teach Critical Race Theory, gender, or anything else that smacked of left political "indoctrination." He'd fire any "Radical Marxist" employed by the Department of Education. He painted anyone as a "Radical Marxist" with the broadest brush. It was anyone who embraced diversity instruction, and especially anyone who advocated transgender inclusion.

He'd demand a rigid separation of gender in sports. He'd certify only those who teach "patriotic" America First values. He'd wipe out teacher tenure, slash the number of school administrators, radically expand school choice, and turn over all major aspects of education policy to parents—

that is those parents who backed "patriotic values." Trump would codify his big education remake plan in what he dubbed a "Parental Bill of Rights."

As Trump put it the idea was to turn back the clock on public education to a narrow 1950s "God and country" patriotism. It would, as he indelicately put it, permanently bar "pink- haired Communists teaching our kids." The end goal was clearly a total ultra-conservative revamp of the education system.

The nation's school districts were the prime target, with the hammer falling hardest on districts in which the majority of students were Black, Hispanic, and lower income. These districts relied heavily on federal Title 1 funding to the tune of nearly twenty billion dollars annually. The money bankrolled such programs as Head Start, free meals, special education programs, and the employment of special ed instructors.

The right had long regarded and resented these programs as wasteful, an onerous use of white middle class tax dollars to subsidize students of color. Any slash in, if not outright elimination of, these federal dollars would result in the loss of vital remedial education programs and services for tens of thousands of students in inner city schools.

If parents and conservative education advocacy groups were allowed to make all the decisions about school district programs and funding use, the result would be catastrophic. They could put constant pressure on local districts and even state officials to opt out of the federally funded programs or recycle the money into programs they consider vital to white middle-class students.

Katherine Dunn, an education equity advocate, underscored the potential devastating damage to public education from this: "Title I and IDEA are the federal government's primary mechanisms to ensure that schools that can't raise much revenue from local property taxes have at least a baseline level of resources."

*****

Trump's planned scrap of the Department of Education was the linchpin in his end goal of turning the schools completely over to conservative advocacy groups. That would ensure that all decisions on programs and funding were made by those in ideological sync with the hard right's demand for "patriotic instruction."

That would sound the death knell for investigations, and the rigorous monitoring, litigation, and negotiating of settlements with school districts that were found in violation of civil rights and equity education requirements. There would be no investigations of sexual discrimination against students or district employees.

There would be no investigation of the wildly disparate discipline policies in many districts that target Black and Hispanic students for suspension or expulsion for even the pettiest of infractions. There would of course be no investigations to determine whether the predominantly Black and Hispanic school districts were being grossly shortchanged in funds received.

Trump's sweeping overhaul of traditional public education would virtually take the word "public" out of "public education." There would not even be a limited role for the federal government, beyond providing funding to be used by conservative education groups any way they saw fit. There would be no remedy for racial or gender discrimination. There would be a wholesale ouster from the classroom and administration ranks of anyone who was deemed liberal or progressive.

The virtual national privatizing of schools would shove education in America back to the narrow, insular, ultra-conservative, flag-waving model of a century ago. That would be an education system and education model that was anything but high-quality, let alone diverse.

4

Impounding the Government

"I will use the president's long-recognized Impoundment Power to squeeze the bloated federal bureaucracy for massive savings. This will be in the form of tax reductions for you. This will help quickly to stop inflation and slash the deficit."
—Trump, from *Agenda 47*

Next to seizing total domination of the SCOTUS and the nation's federal judiciary, ultra-conservatives have had an age-old dream to totally dominate, compartmentalize, and then slash and burn the size, scope, and reach of the federal government. In 2016, Trump was viewed by many in the GOP and rightist groups as the one man who could finally make that dream a reality.

He wasted no time after his presidential election that year in launching a full-throated assault on what the right deemed "big, wasteful government." He shoved through a massive tax giveaway to the wealthy and corporations that starved funding for vital education, jobs, welfare, family support, and heath programs that benefited low to moderate income workers and minorities. In the process, this dug an even deeper hole for the government's revenue debt. He also signed executive orders that weakened environmental and energy regulations.

Trump and the right masked the government assault with appealing populist rhetoric that made it seem like these moves were lowering the debt burden, reducing inflation, cutting bureaucratic red tape, and eliminating waste. These moves would, he claimed, benefit ordinary working-class taxpayers, boost the economy, and strengthen Medicare and Social Security.

In his second term he would ladle out more tax cuts to the rich and corporations, further disempower the government to regulate, and slash spending earmarked for an array of vital government programs. He'd order a total review of all government operations with an eye toward downsizing, if not outright eliminating, many agencies and programs. Trump would accomplish this radical overhaul through the wielding of impoundment. That in effect would snatch from Congress its decision-making authority, especially over the budget and spending, and put it squarely where Trump wanted it, in his own lap.

*****

The use of impoundment by presidents on some spending items was hardly a novel concept for presidents. Specifically, impoundment was the authority of a president to oppose a congressional appropriation for a program or budget item—it refers to when a president refuses to spend funds that Congress has provided for. Trump used that power in 2020 to freeze funding for Ukraine for nearly two months. Eventually, the money was spent.

The issue with presidents, though, was always how and when they could use that authority. The worry was that presidents would abuse that authority. That was certainly the issue and the danger that lawmakers confronted when then-President Richard Nixon used impoundment solely to torpedo programs that he opposed.

At a news conference in July 1973, Nixon was defiant: "I will not spend money if the Congress overspends, and I will not be for programs that will raise the taxes and put a bigger burden on the already overburdened American taxpayer."

He claimed that, as president, the Constitution gave him the right to do as he saw fit with congressionally-approved funding. It didn't. And in response, Congress passed the Congressional Budget and Impoundment and Control Act of 1974 in order to rein in Nixon's abuse of impoundment. Under that law, a president could not unilaterally and permanently kill congressional funding of a program without getting approval from Congress.

The Act was tested when Trump refused to approve the Ukrainian aid money. Trump cited history, saying that presidents as a far back as Thomas Jefferson had used impoundment authority to kill funding for measures they opposed.

The Government Accounting Office did not agree with that view of history. It insisted that Trump exceeded his authority and specifically cited the 1974 congressional Act. "Faithful execution of the law," the GAO noted, "does not permit the President to substitute his own policy priorities for those that Congress has enacted into law."

Trump's goal, like Nixon's, was to put full power over government operations and spending into his own hands. He would then be free to gut federal employment, make all decisions on immigration policy, and dismantle many regulatory agencies. He'd ensure that he had a small army of total loyalists and "yes" men and women to implement any and every one of his policy changes by dumping civil service protections for all employees directly responsible for policy making and implementation. Government employees would now serve at his pleasure.

Trump previewed his plan for wrecking the federal government in October 2020. He signed an executive order that created a new category of civil servants who could be fired and replaced on his whim. When Biden took office, he rescinded the order. During the 2024 presidential campaign he warned, "This MAGA threat is the threat to the brick and mortar of our democratic institutions." Trump made clear he'd demolish both the brick and mortar of those institutions if he got the chance.

*****

Trump's plan to remake the federal government was hardly new. It had been in the playbook of conservatives for decades. Then-President Ronald Reagan got the ball rolling in 1982. He established a commission to improve government efficiency. He assembled more than one hundred private-sector leaders. Their mandate was to "drain the swamp" in Washington.

The group was known as the Grace Commission. It eventually released a forty-seven-volume report with more than two thousand recommendations, including proposals to water down protections for government workers. While it set a working framework for the conservative assault on so-called Big Government, almost none of the proposals were implemented.

Trump would change that by giving himself the power to use impoundment as "a crucial tool with which to obliterate the Deep State, Drain the Swamp, and starve the Warmongers." Noted legal historian Noah Rosenblum opined: "So I think Donald Trump genuinely believed, as he has said, that he had 'an Article II' and that lets him do whatever he wants. And so that being President of the

United States was something like being the monarchical ruler of a kingdom."

He also observed that the Trump end game would be to completely obliterate the Constitutional precept of separation of powers, and independence, "But that's not how the United States government has operated, ever. My first thought was that it seems like he is now trying to put together legal plans that would make the Presidency into more of a kingship and bring it a little bit closer to realizing what he understands the office to be."

Rosenblum's final quip that Trump sought to mold the presidency into what he understands the office to be was much too charitable. Trump was not concerned with understanding the office. His concern was concentrating all federal government decision-making power into his own hands. Impoundment was just one more tool he'd utilize to turn the presidency and the federal government into a personal Trump fiefdom. Trump made sure going into the 2024 presidential election that all understood that goal.

5

The Diversity Assault

"Biden is weaponizing every tool of government power to push this racism and this communism and Marxism. I will instruct the Department of Justice to make clear that any such discrimination is completely and totally illegal, and to investigate the unlawful domination and discrimination and civil right abuses carried out by the Biden administration."
—Trump, from *Agenda 47*

Even by Trump's wildly bold and audacious radical agenda it was shocking. That was Trump calling for something akin to reparations for whites. He was blunt about that in an interview with *Time* in April 2024: "I think there is a definite anti-white feeling in this country and that can't be allowed."

In making this call to redress alleged discrimination against whites, Trump blatantly ripped off the long-standing demand by Black activists for reparations for slavery and past racial discrimination. He vowed to prod Congress to establish a restitution fund for those "unjustly discriminated against by these destructive policies." One of the "destructive policies" he referred to was supposed government favoritism toward minorities and women.

Trump's assault on diversity posed three potentially very damaging consequences. The first was that it openly bolstered the mounting drive by ultra-conservatives to wipe out all diversity, equity, and inclusion (DEI) programs at colleges and in industry, under the guise that these programs discriminated against whites. GOP-led state legislatures took the cue and introduced an avalanche of bills in 2023 to restrict if not outright excise DEI programs in education, state government, contracting, and pension investments.

The second consequence was that if Trump were elected, he could muster the full force of the federal government against DEI programs. His issuance of an executive order, his call to Congress for a restitution fund for whites, and his plan to use the Justice Department to investigate, if not prosecute, any entity that has DEI initiatives in place were ominous indicators of his intent. His vow to create a special team to rapidly review and scrub out all equity programs added even more to the danger.

The third damaging consequence was that it gave credence to the blatant falsity that white men were being systematically shoved out at colleges and the top spots in corporations by minorities and women. This was nothing but a rehash of the ancient self-serving myth that affirmative action discriminated against whites, in that supposedly poorly qualified Blacks and Hispanics got preference over them in hiring and college admissions.

A *USA Today* survey in April 2024 demolished this myth. It again confirmed that white males still made up the vast majority of top management spots at the major corporations, and that minorities and women still wallowed at the lower rungs on the corporate ladder.

*****

In the waning days of his presidency in September 2020, Trump gave a brutal preview of what he intended in his plan to escalate the assault on diversity programs. He signed an executive order that barred any racial sensitivity training by the federal government and government contractors.

That was tantamount to telling contractors that it was no longer necessary to make any effort to have a racially and ethnically diverse workforce as a condition for doing business with the government. That flew squarely in the face of decades of government orders from prior presidents to ensure the elimination of discrimination and exclusion and to promote equity in hiring by companies that contracted with the federal government. Biden also promptly rescinded this order when he took office in January 2021.

In his *Agenda 47* manifesto, Trump cited a checklist of dozens of "equity" initiatives that Biden implemented that supposedly openly discriminated against whites. He further charged, without evidence, that a high-ranking Biden administration official supposedly admitted that the goal was to "re-establish" discrimination against whites in federal programs. He did not identify that official.

Trump took one added swipe at Biden on the issue of diversity: "from day one, Biden has made it his mission to infuse radical policies into the federal government."

By the start of the 2024 presidential campaign, blaming Biden for allegedly racially skewing the federal government toward minorities had become foundational to the Trump campaign's to appeal to angry white voters. The problem with this was that the push for DEI programs did not come on Biden's watch but on Trump's. The impetus was the national revulsion over the murder of George Floyd in May 2020 by a Minneapolis police officer.

Major corporations rushed to publicly reconfirm their commitment to diversity hiring and promotion, and to purge any branding or advertising that could be construed as racially tinged. There was no major public outcry, let alone backlash, against these corporate diversity initiatives.

Trump said nothing about them pro or con during the seven months left in his term. Polls also found that a majority of the public backed the effort to attack "systemic racism." That slowly changed. Ultra-conservatives saw a fresh opening. They reworked their old playbook for assault on affirmative action. DEI programs now became the buzzword for supposed reverse racism and exclusion, not of minorities, but of whites.

The attack produced political results even before the start of the 2024 presidential campaign. More than a few corporations quietly backed away from DEI postings. The fall-off was dramatic. Between November 2020 and November 2021, there was nearly a thirty percent rise in job postings with DEI in the title or description. Between November 2022 and November 2023, the number of postings with DEI in the title or description plunged twenty-three percent.

*****

With Trump and the GOP fully at the helm of federal government policy-making and implementation after the 2024 presidential election, the backsliding by colleges and corporation in regard to diversity initiatives would be in full free fall. They would tread carefully over instituting any new program or firming up support for those already established. They'd fear incurring the wrath of a publicly hostile Trump administration and Trump DOJ toward any special programs to foster DEI. The Heritage Foundation and other influential and well-funded ultra-conservative groups detailed their blueprint for the assault on DEI in a document branded *Project 2025*. This added more teeth to a second Trump administration racial assault. Federal government contractors would no longer be required to comply with anti-discrimination laws. They would not be required to train or promote personnel for diversity. They would not be required to collect any data on racial and ethnic diversity by major companies.

The elimination of virtually all DEI initiatives by corporations and with a Trump-run federal government whip-sawing to get rid of them would assure that America back pedaled to something more like the 1950s, when legal segregation was still the law of the land. National Urban League President Marc Morial underscored the real danger: "They are not advocating for colorblindness. They're advocating for the return of white privilege. They're advocating for the policies that were used during a segregated America." Morial added, "Let's just hide disparities. Let's just pretend they don't exist. Let's sanction things that appear to be race-neutral but are discriminatory."

Morial, if anything, was being too charitable. Trump and the *Project 2025* originators talked little about race-neutral policies. They talked almost exclusively about discrimination against whites, reverse racism, and Trump's special twist—reparations for whites who were allegedly victims of diversity promotion initiatives. In every moment of a Trump second term, this would be the mantra endlessly recited. He'd now have the might of the federal government to ensure it was more than talk.

6

Nine Alitos on the SCOTUS?

"Today's decision... along with other decisions that have been announced recently, were only made possible because I delivered everything as promised, including nominating and getting three highly respected and strong Constitutionalists confirmed to the United States Supreme Court."
—Donald Trump

This was one of the rare times Trump could justifiably and truthfully crow and puff himself up. He had done as he said. He appointed the three SCOTUS justices who put the final nail in the *Roe* coffin.

Trump's braggadocio about his part in packing the Supreme Court of the United States that resulted in the scuttle of *Roe* underscored the monumental role of not just the SCOTUS in shaping law and public policy. It further underscored how SCOTUS decisions have wide ranging effects on law and public policy in America that can extend well into the future.

"We obsess about the modern court for the same reason we obsess about the presidency. During the past century, both institutions have acquired more power at the expense of Congress," observed Jack Shafer, *POLITICO* senior media writer. "Issues that were once a matter of congressional debate and legislation now get commandeered by the president or kicked over to the Supreme Court. With the court amassing more power."

*****

The key to who was the beneficiary of this SCOTUS legal and political prowess and how it was used depended heavily on who sat in the Oval Office. He or she would ultimately decide who would sit on the High Court and what their political leanings and philosophy were. The stakes for this in 2024, as in the past, hinged on who bagged the Oval Office in the 2024 presidential election.

The wildly divergent contrast between Biden and Trump's view of the SCOTUS and judiciary could not have been starker. In a campaign rally in Philadelphia, Pennsylvania to mostly African American supporters in May 2024, Biden publicly pledged, "The next president, they're going to be able to appoint a couple of justices, and I'll be damned—if in fact, we're able to change some of the justices when they retire and put in really progressive judges as we've always had, tell me that won't change your life."

Trump was having none of that. He went one step further in making clear just what type of judge he'd shove on the court if re-elected. The cookie cutter mold for his type of judge was the SCOTUS judge who by 2024 had come to symbolize the most extreme rightwing legal and judicial philosophy of any SCOTUS, even supplanting Clarence Thomas in that category. That was justice Samuel Alito.

Trump gushed over him in a May 2024 tweet: *"Congratulations to United States Supreme Court Justice Samuel Alito for showing the INTELLIGENCE, COURAGE, and "GUTS" to refuse stepping aside from making a decision on anything January 6th related. All U.S. Judges, Justices, and Leaders should have such GRIT - Our Country would be far more advanced than its current status as A BADLY FAILING NATION"*

*****

Trump first issued a challenge on the SCOTUS in his presidential nomination acceptance speech at the Republican Convention in 2016. He made clear where he stood on the exact type of SCOTUS justice he intended to pick and what their judicial philosophy should be. He tossed out the name of the then late ultra-conservative Antonin Scalia during his speech as his kind of judge. This was not simply a double down on his praise of Scalia as the type of judge who, along with Clarence Thomas, would be at the top of his High Court heroes list.

He sent the strongest signal that his picks would not just be garden variety strict constructionists, but activists and influencers on the bench. They would be judges who wouldn't just base their rulings on the standard conservative playbook, but would cajole, hector, and badger other judges to toe the hard conservative line in their rulings—and who would have the gall, when it suited their purpose, not even to try and hide it. He reiterated that hard-nosed sentiment in verbally back-slapping Alito in his social media tweet in May 2024.

It was no accident that with Scalia gone from the court after his death in February 2018, that for a moment it looked almost like a moderate court in some of its rulings on abortion rights, affirmative action, voting rights, and the feds paying for contraceptives at religious hospitals. The outcome would have almost certainly been different if Scalia and more conservatives had sat on the court bench.

In decades past, many justices—both Democratic- and Republican-appointed—had scrapped party loyalties and based their legal decisions solely on the merit of the law, constitutional principles, and the public good. But Scalia was a judicial horse of a different color.

The tip-off that judges like him would vote their ideology rather than the law came from George W. Bush. On the presidential campaign trail in 2000, Bush was asked, if elected what kind of judge he'd look for and nominate. He didn't hesitate. He pledged to appoint "strict constructionists" to the court and specifically named Thomas, Scalia, and William Rehnquist as the judges that perfectly fit that description.

By then the three had already carved out a hardline niche as three of the most reflexive, knee-jerk, reactionary jurists to grace the court in decades. Their votes to torpedo, water down, eviscerate, or erode equal rights on all issues from abortion to civil rights were so predictable they could have been mailed in.

*****

A Supreme Court justice can sit on the court for years, even decades, and watch as legions of Republicans and Democrats come and go in Congress and the White House. All the while, they are shaping and remaking law and public policy for decades to come with their votes, rulings, and opinions. A Trump win in 2024 would guarantee that those votes, rulings, and opinions would reflect, with only slight variation, the hardcore conservative position on the issues.

There are two prime examples. The first was in respect to racial matters. More specifically, affirmative action and racially skewed redistricting. The court would almost certainly eliminate completely the last vestige of attempts by schools and corporations to set guidelines for enhancing racial equity. The court would likewise reject many of the cases that were brought to end discriminatory redistricting, especially in the South where Blacks were the majority in many congressional districts.

The second example was religion. More specifically, the use of public facilities and public monies by religious institutions. Private groups and conservative religious educational groups had long demanded the unhampered use of public facilities for religious worship, activities, and programs.

They were just as vociferous in demanding that taxpayers foot the bill for this use. The court almost certainly would grant them their wish. That would completely obliterate the line between church and state—a line that had been badly eroded in prior rulings by the SCOTUS and other courts.

These were just two issues that a Trump refashioned SCOTUS would likely do his bidding on. There were many other cases that would come before the SCOTUS during a Trump second term that the justices would flex their ideological muscle on, all in line with Trump and far right conservatives whose avowed aim was to reshape government in their political image. Trump would have one other advantage in how he acted with the SCOTUS during a second term.

He already had a plurality of justices who were ideologically attuned to his agenda. He wouldn't make the mistake of over-reaching too quickly on getting the justices to do his bidding. He'd frame his change proposals carefully within the power that the Constitution grants the president. Several justices, starting with Chief Justice John Roberts, had dropped hints that they favored a broad interpretation of the powers of the president.

During the 2024 presidential campaign Trump faced multiple criminal indictments. The SCOTUS grappled with whether Trump could claim absolute immunity from prosecution for acts deemed illegal that were committed within and without the scope of the presidency.

However, even by the politically accommodating standard of the SCOTUS conservative majority, it would have been an indefensible stretch to hand Trump absolute power. That would have stretched to the outer limit the right of a president, in or out of office, to break the law and not be held legally accountable. Yet, in a stunning decision the High Court did just. It ruled that Trump and any other presidents had almost free license to commit illegal acts under the highly elastic guise of executive immunity.

In fact, when the court agreed to accept Trump's appeal for absolute immunity, this signaled that Roberts and undoubtedly one or more of the other ultra-conservatives on the court were open to Trump's pitch for complete legal absolution. Even if the court ultimately rejected Trump's absurd claim of total immunity, which it didn't, it still represented a victory for him.

The debate over the issue, the endless motions filed, the opinions presented by all sides were grueling and time consuming. It gave credence to the ridiculous notion that a president, even when out of office, had a free pass to commit any crime with the full knowledge that he was shielded from any criminal liability.

In the short term, the SCOTUS debate on Trump's absolute immunity claim killed any chance that the criminal cases against him would start before the November election. That was a de facto gift of immunity and a de facto upholding of total executive power for the moment.

A legal expert involved in the case made the grim point that "Trump's first preference would be a ruling that he is immune, but a second preference would be a ruling that there is some kind of complicated factual test for immunity, so it has to be remanded. If, but more likely when that happened, the case would get bogged down on questions about to what extent each of the four counts in the indictment rest on official acts of the then-president, which might be protected." The court ruling in Trump's favor ensured that that would be the case.

*****

There was no other way to characterize the SCOTUS in 2024 than as a Trump SCOTUS. It was a court that in varying legalistic ways was deeply committed to aid and abet much of Trump's conservative remake of law and public policy. It would have plenty of opportunities in the wide range of compelling issues and cases it would decide in a second Trump term—all of which would have profound impact on the shape of American society for possibly decades after Trump left office.

7

Drill, Baby, Drill

"As President, I will set a national goal of ensuring that America has the No. 1 lowest cost of energy of any industrial country anywhere on Earth. We will not only match China we will be cheaper than China by a lot. And more energy will mean lower inflation that will mean more jobs."
—Trump, from *Agenda 47*

The meeting was supposed to be hush-hush and exclusively private. But word quickly leaked out about it, and for good reason. Trump in a private meeting at Mar-a-Lago in April 2024 bluntly demanded that the twenty executives present from the top oil industry conglomerates, among them Chevron, Exxon, and Occidental Petroleum, cough up the staggering campaign contribution sum of one billion dollars to his campaign.

Trump told the executives that the one billion dollars he demanded was virtually peanuts compared to the bountiful riches they'd get in return if he was re-elected. He'd roll back every Biden executive order limiting or restricting drilling on public lands. He'd get the U.S. again out of the Paris Accords to limit fossil fuel use, and kill the expansion of green energy use. He'd guarantee that the oil and gas industry continued to get more than one hundred billion in tax breaks at the very least.

Senate and House Democrats were apoplectic at news of the meeting and the proposed deal. They demanded answers from the oil executives about the meeting and the promises Trump made to feather their nest with eye-popping tax breaks and unlimited drilling rights:

> "Time and time again, both Mr. Trump and the U.S. oil and gas industry have proved they are willing to sell out Americans to pad their own pockets," Senators Ron Wyden of Oregon and Sheldon Whitehouse of Rhode Island jibed. "And now, emboldened by impunity, Mr. Trump and Big Oil are flaunting their indifference to U.S. citizens' economic well-being for all to see, conferring on how to trade campaign cash for policy changes. Such potential abuses must be scrutinized."

Trump predictably fired back. "President Trump is supported by people who share his vision of American energy dominance to protect our national security, and bring down the cost of living for all Americans," noted Trump campaign spokesperson Karoline Leavitt.

Whether Trump was just bloviating to the executives or really did expect to get that big a bundle of cash from the oil industry, it still smacked of a classic quid pro quo, play for pay, taken to the audacious, even the outrageous, outer limit. But more frightfully important, it gave a stark preview of what Trump had in mind for America's energy future and more particularly who the big winners and losers would be in a second Trump administration.

*****

Beyond the massive tax breaks for the oil and gas industry, Trump said he'd get rid of all the prohibitions to drilling, which was the jewel-in-the-crown give-away to the industry. He'd further scrap the moratorium on gas exports. He'd then eliminate all regulations to cut down on automotive pollution. This was a bountiful gift package of which Trump rightly said that if even a fraction of it were enacted, it would be worth tens of billions to the industry.

Trump did not say it, but the implication was that if Biden got back in office, all of that industry largesse Trump promised would be off the table. That could even include the tens of billions in tax breaks it already was getting. That possibility had to be uppermost in the minds of the oil industry magnates who flocked to Mar-a-Lago to hear Trump's pitch for a billion in campaign cash.

Trump was emboldened to make the head-turning one-billion-dollar campaign shakedown from them for two good reasons. The first was that it was not a new shakedown demand. In his 2020 presidential campaign, he tossed out what could only be called a bribe solicitation.

He floated the idea that he'd be open to grant Exxon Oil drilling permits if the company coughed up a twenty-five-million-dollar donation. He then quickly pretended that it was something akin to a joke by immediately saying that if he did that, he'd be "totally compromised." But was he really just jesting and would he really be bothered about being compromised if Exxon had believed him and tried to take him up on his illegal offer?

The second reason for his bold shakedown demand of the industry was that the companies had already shelled out millions to Trump's reelection campaign. By contrast, the industry donated a paltry half million to the Biden campaign chest. The added billions that the oil and gas executives gave to Trump's 2024 campaign was a huge boost from their contributions to his 2016 and even his 2020 campaigns.

They got more than their money's worth each time. He enacted a series of industry-friendly policies, including nominating then-ExxonMobil CEO Rex Tillerson as his secretary of state. He OKed drilling in Alaska's Arctic National Wildlife Refuge, sped up the review process for drilling projects under the National Environmental Policy Act, and ultimately reversed more than one hundred environmental regulations.

"Biden constantly throws a wet blanket to the oil and gas industry," Dan Eberhart, a Trump donor and CEO of an oil-field services company said. "Trump's 'drill, baby, drill' philosophy aligns much better with the oil patch than Biden's green-energy approach. It's a no-brainer."

******

Trump's "drill, baby, drill" pledge to the oil industry company heads was simple and to the point. He left no doubt exactly how he would fully cater to the industry's wants. But the admonition was more than just a pitch man's adage; it reflected the long-standing war that the oil and gas industry had waged against any effort by the government to impose rigorous environmental standards and regulations on the major companies' oil and gas operations.

The major issue under during Obama's and then Biden's White House tenures was the federal government's effort rein in unfettered drilling on public lands. That entailed enacting new restrictions and tightening old ones on the issuance of federal drilling permits and leases.

Trump promised to end virtually all of the restrictions. He and the industry always couched their demand for the cease and desist of regulations with the argument that they hurt consumers by drastically increasing oil and gas prices. The oil executives claimed it was not a profit grab on their part, as critics insisted, but a noble effort to lower energy costs, create jobs, and tamp down inflation. This would, the industry and Trump assured, be a huge boon to the economy.

In his *Agenda 47* manifesto, Trump argued that ending drilling restrictions would "unleash American oil and natural gas production and free up the vast stores of liquid gold on America's public land for energy development." Trump further assured that the other big payoff in ending drilling restrictions was that it would guarantee America's energy independence.

During his first term, Trump gave a fulsome preview of just what he had in store on the energy front for the country if re-elected. He was almost a one-man environmental protection wrecking crew. Environmental experts ticked off more than one hundred environmental protective measures that Trump either watered down or outright repealed. That didn't include at least a dozen more rules that he would have eliminated if he had had more time in office.

The rules covered the gamut of protective regulations for water pollution, air pollution and emissions, wildlife protection, toxic chemicals and substances, drilling and extraction, infrastructure and planning, and power plants. Trump's argument never changed. Federal regulatory agencies, such as the Environmental Protection Agency and the Department of the Interior in particular, had way overstepped their mandate with their allegedly crippling regulations.

In every instance that Trump gutted a regulation, he covered himself by claiming that the measure would free the oil and gas industry to provide more and presumably cheaper energy supplies. Even more incredibly, he claimed that at the same time it would make the air, water, and land even cleaner.

Trump's agency spokespersons didn't say exactly how tossing more carbon in the air through unchecked drilling would make the air cleaner. But then again, that wasn't the point anyway. The point was merely to pander to the fabulously rich industry that regarded the right to drill wherever it pleased as practically a sacred rite.

Trump's environmental opponents of course begged to differ and insisted that the air would be dirtier, and the water and land more contaminated, and that would result in the sickness and death for thousands from poor air and water quality.

The greatest immediate threat to health and safety that most experts agreed upon was global warning. The proven culprit without doubt was the oil and gas industry and its massive fossil fuel emissions that were the prime reason for the Earth's soaring temperatures. In a report in June 2024, the United Nations zeroed in on the potential environmental debacle that global warming posed. It warned of continuing torrid temperatures and heat waves, and starkly predicted if that continued, "Beyond that point the impacts of climate change could get even more dangerous for people and critical ecosystems than what's already happened."

*****

Environmental protection advocacy groups fought back against Trump's environmental assault during his term. They would likely fight back just as hard against it in a Trump second term. In the first term they filed countless lawsuits, court challenges, and appeals to block Trump's regulatory wipeout. In more than a few cases, they were successful.

One notable example was a federal appeals court decision that overturned a Trump order that damped down the Obama administration-imposed controls on carbon dioxide emissions from coal and natural gas-burning power plants. The court's decision confirmed to Trump that the agency badly overstepped its legal authority under the Clean Air Act to reduce carbon pollution.

Another prime issue and bone of contention was the grab of public lands for unlimited, uncontrolled oil and gas drilling. Millions of acres were controlled by the federal government that had either proven or suspected vast storehouses of oil and gas deposits buried deep. They were ripe for the industry's picking.

There were two Trump measures, in particular, to undo the blockage of the companies to drill without checks that were indicative of the intensity of the industry to get unrestricted access to the public land. And at the same time, these stirred the equally intense fight by environmentalists to stop the giveaway.

The first revised and partially repealed an Obama-era rule limiting methane emissions on public lands. That included the intentional venting and flaring from drilling operations. In July 2020, a federal court struck down the revision, calling the Trump administration's reasoning "wholly inadequate." It mandated enforcement of the original rule. However, the Obama-era rule was later partially struck down in a separate court case, during which the Trump administration declined to defend it. The court acted after a prompt filing against it by a coalition of environmental groups.

The other was Trump's directive to shorten the time required for review and possible approval of public infrastructure projects, such as roads, pipelines, and telecommunications networks, all regulated under the nation's environmental flagship National Environmental Policy Act.

Trump's ruling slashed the time it would take for completing environmental studies. It also limited which kinds of projects could be reviewed and scrapped any requirement for review by federal regulatory agencies of the damage or potential damage that an oil and gas industry project could do to the environment, the most worrisome being climate change.

Biden restored as many of the regulatory controls as possible. Biden repeatedly made clear that Trump's deregulation assault did irreparable harm to the environment and endangered public health and safety.

In April 2024, EPA Director Michael Regan, with the blessing of Biden, underscored the threat by noting, "President Biden understands the threat that 'forever chemicals' pose to the health of families across the country. That's why EPA launched its PFAS Strategic Roadmap, a whole-of-agency approach to protecting public health and addressing the harm to communities overburdened by PFAS pollution. Designating these chemicals under our Superfund authority will allow EPA to address more contaminated sites, take earlier action, and expedite cleanups, all while ensuring polluters pay for the costs to clean up pollution threatening the health of communities."

This was the exact kind of response and action to correct environmental damage that Trump and his oil and gas industry backers were determined to undo as quickly as possible if he got back into office.

*****

Two other major differences would characterize a second Trump White House tenure from his first in his assault on energy and environmental regulations. It would be even more extreme and more perilous because it would be more focused. Trump's *Agenda 47* proposal on energy production was one tip-off of that.

It was by far the longest, most detailed, and hardest-hitting attack on Biden's energy policy. A Trump spokesperson underscored Trump's greater knowledge of how to hit the ground running the second time: "The president will benefit from having the experience of being in office before, he'll get a faster head start on his agenda. He won't be encumbered by the need to be re-elected, so there will be a short window of time, but he may be more aggressive as a result."

Yet another Trump spokesperson reiterated that point. "He will undo everything [Joe] Biden has done, he will move more quickly and go further than he did before," said Myron Ebell, who headed the EPA transition team for

Trump's first term. "He will act much more expeditiously to impose his agenda."

Trump and the oil and gas industry had a special target in a second Trump term that was barely on the table his first term. That was the issue of green energy. Biden proposed billions in spending for an array of green and clean energy projects, with a special emphasis on a massive expansion in the use of electric vehicles. Congress passed Biden's legislative package with no Republican votes.

The legislation created a lot of new jobs in solar, wind, and battery manufacturing. That posed a major challenge to the oil and gas industry. It was enraged and vowed to reverse the clean energy spending priority. Trump would fully back that effort once he returned to the White House.

Carla Sands, a key environment adviser to the pro-Trump America First Policy Institute went further and branded Biden's green energy initiatives "apocalyptic green fantasies." Trump's first line of attack to skirt Congress would be to try to use executive orders to again whittle away at the tax credits earmarked for solar, wind, and electric manufacturing projects. His second line of attack would be to try and put every one of his own energy and environmental deregulation measures back into force again. That certainly included snubbing his nose again at the Paris climate agreement.

*****

The second major difference in a Trump second term would be that he would have the almost total freedom and the leisure to handpick the most extreme anti-environmental personnel to do his hatchet-job bidding on all environmental regulations. During the first Trump term there were, at least by Trump's standard, some individuals who served as a partial brake on Trump going full bore and trying to round-file every environmental regulation. That might even have included a hard push to get rid of the EPA entirely. He didn't quite go that far. However, he did everything possible to water down the EPA's regulatory reach.

Andrew Rosenberg, a former National Oceanic and Atmospheric Administration official, made that point: "There were people—part of a reasonable mainstream in his first term who buffered against his craziest instincts—they won't be there anymore."

Also, the slash and burn environmental plan Trump laid out in *Agenda 47* was not the only environmental assault plan he could lean on. There was also the far-right Heritage Foundation's *Project 2025*. In its section on energy and environment it flatly said that the EPA and the Department of Interior needed to be whittled down to almost, if not complete, extinction.

Trump almost certainly would stock his administration with those affiliated with the foundation. They confirmed in stark and terrifying language exactly how they'd be among the top echelon of a second Trump administration's guiding lights. "We are writing a battle plan, and we are marshaling our forces," insisted Paul Dans, director of *Project 2025*. "Never before has the whole conservative movement banded together to systematically prepare to take power day one and deconstruct the administrative state."

The U.S. is still the globe's second biggest carbon polluter. With Trump unrestrained in his assault on environmental regulations, the U.S. would almost certainly contribute an even greater amount of carbon pollution to the Earth's atmosphere. For the four years of a Trump second term, and even after, this would sound the death knell for the efforts to curb deadly global heating.

There would be more intense heat waves, more deadly weather extremes that would intensify floods, droughts, hurricanes, cyclones, rising ocean levels, and the further erosion of the polar ice caps and the ozone layer. Scientists repeatedly warned that the world must cut greenhouse emissions drastically and eliminate them entirely by 2050, to avoid breaching agreed-upon temperature limits. Violating that would pose catastrophic environmental dangers to billions of people globally. The Trump plan did nothing to help avoid that peril and everything to ensure that the environmental nightmare scientists warn of became the Earth's future reality.

There was no mystery why Trump made energy policy a keystone of his plan to take back the White House in 2024. The energy industry had the money. It showed that it was willing to spend it lavishly on Trump.

Even more, energy policy was the one issue that had the potential to be a voter attention-getter. Trump and the energy industry could peddle the notion that dumping the supposedly onerous job-hindering environmental regulations, which also raised gas prices at the pump and fuel costs, would be an economic boon for the nation and a huge cost savings for consumers.

It was a classic case of dollars overriding for many the monumental potential short- and long-term damage to the environment and public health that unfettered drilling posed. That mattered little to Trump and the oil executives. They would continue to cheer his "drill, baby, drill."

8

Peace Through Strength

"Less than three years ago, I'd fully rebuilt the United States military and steered America into such a strong global position. That peace was breaking out all over the world, we had peace through strength."
—Trump, from *Agenda 47*

Trump's oft-stated claim that peace was everywhere and that it was attained through American military might was flowery and brash, but like much else from Trump it was also misleading. On the surface, Trump could rightfully boast that during his four years in office there was no major war being fought and no slaughter that almost always is the gruesome feature of a brutal civil war somewhere.

On the surface, Trump's plan for a strong military and a peaceful world was straightforward. He'd spend lavishly on the military. But it wouldn't just be a case of tossing unlimited dollars at the military. He'd also make sure that the dollars spent were not wasted—that they went to buy and equip the latest in weaponry, technology, and top-notch personnel recruitment and training.

He'd demand that European nations pay back an estimated two hundred billion dollars spent on weaponry for Ukraine in its war against Russia. He'd move quickly to make the military an attractive option for young men and women to join. He maintained that almost no one wants to join the military anymore because it was riddled with a left-wing political correctness philosophy that allegedly weakened and corrupted the military and made it a laughingstock.

He was emphatic on that point: "I will restore the proud culture and honor traditions of America's armed forces. And there will be no Marxism allowed, no communism allowed, and we'll get rid of the fascists."

*****

Trump's hard-nosed promise to rebuild the military fit neatly into his narrative that the military was a tower of power during his four years in office and because of that there were no wars anywhere. When he made that nearly identical pledge during the 2016 presidential campaign, it resonated with many voters and got him a lot of votes. A lot of those votes came from the troops. Nearly fifty percent of them had a far greater liking for him than their commander in chief, outgoing President Obama.

Trump was given relatively high marks though for providing greater funding for military research and development. The goal was to ensure that the military kept pace with China and Russia on the latest technological changes. In Trump's eyes, the emphasis must always be on full military preparedness.

But as for Trump's widely self-touted claim that the world was a haven of peace for his four years, it was anything but that. There were four wars raging, in Afghanistan, Syria, Iraq, and Yemen, and the U.S. had a direct hand in all of them with troops, advisors, or military support to one faction or another in these wars.

Trump did nothing to end the U.S. involvement, let alone the fighting. Nevertheless, that didn't stop him from making this claim in January 2024 at a *Fox News* Townhall: "I had no wars. I'm the only president in 72 years... I didn't have any wars." That was the misleading picture Trump painted about his alleged success in maintaining a totally peaceful world during his term.

Trump's tout of his supposed spotless no-wars record wasn't the only thing dubious about his relationship with America's military. Trump was unabashed in his aim of turning the military into a political weapon. The time-tested unwritten rule was that the military would not engage in any political maneuvering or interference.

This unstated prohibition has held from the time of America's founding. The prohibition was meant to ensure all government policy decisions, especially on the always crucial issues of war and peace, were made by civilians. The aim was to avoid the perils of military control and dictatorship. It was in effect an unwritten separation of powers.

Trump tried to upend that prohibition in several ways. One was to butt into military criminal justice proceedings and findings against servicemen and women who committed crimes, particularly war crimes. He pardoned several offenders. "They were not close calls on the merits," Aaron O'Connell a Marine Corps officer who served in Afghanistan and in Obama's National Security Council noted. "Why get involved with this? It only hurts the military, hurts the rule of law and hurts the image of the U.S. as a law-abiding nation."

Next, after civil unrest erupted in several cities following the murder of George Floyd by a Minneapolis police officer in 2020, Trump repeatedly threatened to send in the army to restore law and order. He contended that he had to use the army because supposedly liberal politically correct Democratic mayors in those cities were doing nothing to stop the anarchy in their cities.

The top military brass almost to a person opposed the use of the military for what was clearly the job of local law enforcement. It was butting in, not just a case of egoistic meddling. The greatest danger if Trump had gotten his way in the use of military to quell a domestic disturbance was that it would have radically changed the entire nature of the historic function of the military.

"Trump's willingness to use the military against legitimate protests in America [last] year stands out as particularly significant and damaging," noted Carter Malkasian, a former senior Defense Department official. "The backlash was thankfully great, so hopefully our institutions have emerged undamaged."

*****

Trump had yet another radical plan to upend the traditional military role. He'd send them to the U.S./Mexican border and put them to work policing that border and even aiding in the construction of his roundly criticized and controversial border wall. Immigration control was, of course, a purely civilian policy matter.

Trump was undaunted. He relentlessly demanded that a sizable portion of the Pentagon budget be diverted to the construction of the wall and the deployment of troops on the border to stop the rush of illegal immigrants into the country. "I think Congress will need to rethink many of the provisions it routinely puts into law," observed Todd Harrison, a budget expert at the Center for Strategic and International Studies, "that allow the president to reallocate certain types of funding in a crisis without prior approval from Congress."

Trump also was determined to tout his administration and himself as the presidency that restored a supposedly weak, depleted, demoralized, leftist political tainted military back to world-class greatness and respect. His son, Donald Jr. wrote a tweet in October 2020 declaring mission accomplished by his dad on that score: "Trump properly funded our military after Obama-Biden decimated it."

Trump Jr.'s claim that liberal Democrat Obama in essence wrecked the military simply echoed his father's oft-repeated claim. He pointed to funding as proof that Obama starved the military of funding and support.

This was a falsehood. Obama, as other presidents routinely did, significantly bumped up military spending. During his first four years the amount spent soared to over three trillion dollars. Trump spent much less than that during his term. The Obama military budget spending rendered the Trump myth of a sagging, underfunded, unprepared military, just that, a myth.

Trump's great boast that he was the president who finally ended the nearly two-decade long fruitless occupation and war in Afghanistan came with a huge qualifier. He did broker the deal with the Taliban for the withdrawal of U.S. forces from the country. However, the withdrawal was messy, chaotic, and provided no mechanisms for monitoring and oversight to assure that the Taliban complied with the terms of the agreement on withdrawal.

The predictable happened. The Taliban did what it wanted after the U.S withdrawal. By then Trump was out of office and he took no responsibility for the resulting chaos. Yet he could boast that he had fulfilled his campaign pledge to end the U.S. engagement there and that was enough.

However, Trump took every opportunity he could to rail at Biden as the cause of the messy U.S. withdrawal. His big moment for the Biden blame game came during the June 2024 presidential debate with Biden. He railed, "He was so bad with Afghanistan. It was such a horrible embarrassment. Most embarrassing moment in the history of our country."

In a report a year earlier, in April 2023, Biden fired back at Trump's criticism of the Afghan withdrawal handling. He blamed the slipshod bungle on "neglect," "deliberate degradation, "a depleted operation," and a non-existent "transition process."

Trump, though, would never allow an unpleasant reality to spoil the illusory image he crafted of himself as the great peacemaker. By the end of Trump's term, the fawning that the military brass and soldiers had for him initially had clearly plunged. His approval rating among the troops dropped nearly ten percent. There was much talk among military analysts, probably charitably, that his legacy for handling the military would be problematic.

Retired Admiral James Stavridis, the former top officer at NATO, was one of these analysts. He said that Trump would have "a very mixed legacy. He was a strong advocate for funding the Pentagon and the Department of Veterans Affairs, but his crude language, his pardoning of war criminals and his sudden removal of troops will be remembered negatively."

Trump's naked effort to politicize an institution that from the country's founding was grounded firmly on the principle of having no political involvement was deeply troubling. This meddling saddled the military within and without with a confounding dilemma over its image and mission and even its existence.

Undaunted, Trump as usual placed the blame for an allegedly decrepit military on Biden: "Then, as I work to again rebuild America's military strength and deterrence that Joe Biden so foolishly squandered." Beyond the Biden blame game, there was every indication in Trump's ringing pronouncements on rebuilding the military that there would be even more tampering, obstructionism, and boasting about his alleged restoration of the military. In the end, he'd keep his word and plow loads more money into the military, while making sure it would do his bidding, not the nation's.

Or as Retired Admiral James Stavridis put it, "Strategically, the military will remember him as a very political commander in chief."

9

Anything Goes—Deregulating America

"Cutting wasteful and job-killing regulations was a key part of my America First economic agenda that built the greatest economy in the history of the world. As I work to quickly save America from Joe Biden's economic disaster—and that's what it is, one of the great economic disasters of all time—I will restore my famously successful executive order requiring that for everyone NEW regulation, two OLD regulations must be eliminated—and I will ask Congress to make it permanent."
—Trump, from *Agenda 47*

A slew of former Trump officials, as well as those who hoped to be Trump officials if he was reelected in 2024, all ticked off their bucket lists of governmental agencies and regulations to go after in a series of interviews. Once in office, they'd water down, rework, or out and out eliminate them. Banking, the environment, workplace safety, oil and gas drilling, consumer protection, Wall Street securities—all topped a seemingly endless list of regulatory rules that would get the hatchet treatment.

This was, of course, all in line with their former, or hoped-to-be future, boss' loud and long-stated plan to hack away at everything that supposedly hindered growth, the economy, and job creation. Robert Bowers, a former Trump official, typified the rush to fall in line with Trump on regulation. He called the Securities and Exchange Commission an "unaccountable meddling shakedown agency" that "uses its regulation to target political enemies, to ram through woke and radical green agenda."

Trump had to glow at that type of language and the assault on the SEC. He didn't just assault with deregulation. He spelled out what would change or go. He'd end any independence that regulatory agencies, such as the FCC and the FTC, had and put them directly under his control. He'd review every old and new regulation with a hard eye toward scrapping or watering it down. He'd put a firm spending cap on all governmental regulatory agencies. He'd require all government regulations to be posted publicly. He'd prohibit regulators from any enforcement action without his saying so.

He'd demand that all civil service employees be retested. This had nothing to do with furthering their knowledge of and training in civil service procedures. It was a giant step toward fulfillment of Trump's oft stated goal of putting civil service government employees directly under his control as employees who serve at the pleasure of the president, in this case Trump. Said Trump, "We will put unelected bureaucrats back in their place, liberate the U.S. economy, and attract millions of jobs and trillions of dollars to our shores."

*****

Trump got a fairly good start during his first term in laying the groundwork for his goal of an almost "anything goes" for all American industries, with no government agencies butting in to tell then what they could and couldn't do. His hatchet job during his term on more than one hundred environmental protection and safety rules was a strong testament to that. Biden quickly reversed many of Trump's damaging rule changes.

However, Trump's rework of the rules and Biden's scrap of them showed just how precarious a rule can be when faced with a president who has the power of the executive pen. Trump did not need congressional approval to go after the EPA and environmental protective regulations. He did it on his authority alone.

The other saving grace then, and many opponents hoped it would be again in the event of another Trump term, was the courts. The damage to public health and safety that Trump's deregulation changes would have had if they had come into full effect would have been devastating. Fortunately, the courts stepped in and put on hold or struck down nearly eighty percent of Trumps' environmental rule changes. They also in most cases thwarted his efforts to end the legislative process and suspend rules that were already in effect.

That was Trump's first term. Much of the federal judiciary thanks to Trump's judicial appointments, particularly the SCOTUS, moved to the right. They would be far more likely in a second Trump term to look with much less favor on the avalanche of challenges Trump would get from environmental groups, consumer protection advocates, labor unions, and other industry watchdog groups.

*****

There were more clues as to what to expect, beyond the most publicized EPA assault, in other areas where Trump aimed to wipe away regulations. The first was the amount of spending Trump put into regular regulatory monitoring and enforcement. The estimated sum was ten billion dollars. That was paltry compared to the more than one hundred billion dollars that Obama spent on regulatory enforcement. It was also almost paltry compared to the more than forty billion dollars that conservative GOP president George W. Bush put into regulation oversight.

While it was true that courts tossed out the majority of Trump's deregulatory orders, about one quarter of them still were upheld. That meant that Trump did attain much of his stated goal, even when he suffered defeat in court, which was to eviscerate the Obama administration's regulatory toughening measures.

One example cited was the Clean Power Plan. Obama unveiled it publicly in August 2015. It tightened the standard for gas emissions from power plants. Trump sought to scrap the plan. Though the courts ultimately upheld the Obama order, the EPA, now under fire from Trump, revised the rules to soften the standard. The court's knock down of Trump's reversal, together with the EPA revising the rules on emissions, left enforcement hanging. It was not clear what the precise standard was.

A closer look at Trump's orders which the courts sustained painted a different and more dangerous picture of how Trump could dismantle the regulatory apparatus. The Brookings Institute, in an exhaustive study of Trump's deregulatory onslaught, found that out of thirty cases in which Trump tried to reverse Obama's executive tougher regulatory orders, he was either partially or fully successful in twenty-seven of the cases.

Of forty cases in which Trump tried to put a totally new rule in place not connected to anything Obama did, he was either partially or fully successful in thirty-four of the cases. What, then, appeared to be a losing effort by Trump to gut regulatory enforcement was anything but that when fine-tuned with the number of wins he scored.

Then there was the Strengthening Transparency in Regulatory Science Rule or the "Secret Science" rule, that the courts upheld. This would give a new administration authority to scrap or reshape any regulatory rule it desired, in any way it wanted. Trump would also have full authority to suspend enforcement of a rule while a court decided the inevitable legal challenge to it. That amounted to scrapping enforcement for an indefinite period.

The two regulatory agencies that Trump almost certainly would put at the top of his hit list during his second term would again be the EPA and the Department of the Interior. They were especially vulnerable for another reason. In his first term Trump was phenomenally successful in getting either partial or full wins, or lengthy delays, in their final rulings.

Trump was able to compile his not inconsiderable wins on his regulations gutting with courts that he had not yet packed with a slew of ideological hardnosed conservatives. That most importantly included the SCOTUS. That would not be the case in a second term. He would have a much more favorable judicial climate in the federal courts and the SCOTUS when he again got the avalanche of challenges from consumer, environmental, and labor advocacy groups to his wave of regulation elimination orders.

Trump's final ace card would be the same one that Biden used to get rid of Trump's orders. He could order the heads of all the regulatory agencies to conduct a full review of all regulatory enhancements and the rules of his that were reversed by Biden. He'd have the agency heads target them for removal.

Biden understood the mortal threat that Trump would again pose to the nation's regulatory machinery. In the months before the 2024 presidential election started, he proposed a rash of new regulations that firmed up enforcement—just in case. Vice President Harris, who replaced Biden as Trump's Democratic presidential opponent, would defend those regulations and Biden's environmental protection program during the campaign and afterwards if elected. It was that fact that gave Trump even more grist for the attack mill. "President Trump will not be deterred from rolling back Joe Biden's costly, burdensome and dumb regulations," insisted Karoline Keavitt, the national press secretary for Trump's campaign. "He will do what's best for the American people, no matter how long it takes."

Given Trump's full-bore assault on regulations his first term, this was anything but an idle threat.

10

"The Greatest Economy in History!"

"I built the greatest economy in the history of the world. In fact, I did it twice when you think about it, and now we will have to do it again. "
—Trump, from *Agenda 47*

There were two themes that Trump repeatedly hammered on at practically every stop during the 2024 presidential campaign. One was that Biden had turned America into a wide-open gate that let countless numbers of dangerous, crime-prone illegal immigrants into the country.

The other was that during his term he engineered the greatest economic boom in American history. After crowing that dubious claim, he quickly added his standard follow-up set-piece to blame Biden: "Joe Biden has been a disaster for the economy. Between his massive tax hikes, his anti-energy crusade, and his trillions of dollars in wasteful spending, Biden caused the highest inflation in almost half a century." When Biden dropped out of the race in July 2024, Trump pivoted quickly, without missing a beat, and ripped his now-opponent Harris for allegedly wrecking the economy while on the Biden team.

Trump quickly added one more boast—that if re-elected, the economic good times would roll even bigger, faster, better, and longer. In short, under a Trump second administration America would be transformed into the proverbial economic land of milk and honey for all.

He'd accomplish that magical feat this way. He'd hack away at those pesky and cumbersome regulations. He'd junk Biden's tax hikes on corporations and the wealthy. He'd then turn around and give them back their boundless tax breaks.

*****

There were two major questions about Trump's boast that he built the greatest economy in the history of the world. One, how true was it? Two, could he really work the economic miracle he claimed if he got a second term?

First, the claim about America's economy under his watch being the greatest ever. Without getting yet into the specifics to determine fact from fiction about it, mouthing it as "the greatest ever" was pure campaign stump hyperbole, as Trump intended it to be.

So, based on the usual economic metrics of growth, sustainability, and performance how much truth was there that Trump did preside over a healthy economy? And how exactly did he make it such?

The number one indicator of the health of an economy is the employment rate. On this Trump's claim of a robust economy had some merit. Joblessness did plunge to the lowest it had been since the 1950s. But as usual with Trump's claims, there was a huge caveat. The economic recovery began and gained a full head of steam during the second Obama term. The jobless numbers were a prime example.

Each month during Obama's second term the total number of new jobs added topped two hundred thousand. By contrast, during Trump's term the jobless number monthly was slightly greater than one hundred and eighty thousand.

Many economists branded the economic surge during Trump's term as the Obama recovery. The recovery factors were characterized by record low interest rates, housing market recovery, increased business start-ups, greater corporate investment in technology and expansion, and a stable financial banking and financial markets industry. All were in full force during Obama's second term. Trump was in the right place at the right time when he took office in 2017. He benefited from the upward economic trends and then promptly took full credit for them.

The second leading measure of a nation's economic growth is the strength of the nation's GDP. During Trump's term, the growth numbers were mediocre, so mediocre that they lagged behind the GDP growth numbers during both the Obama and George W. Bush administrations.

The third leading indicator is wage increases. They did grow under Trump. But they also grew steadily during Obama's second term. When adjusted for inflation, they were much less than in the 1960s.

The fourth leading indicator is the federal deficit. It continued to balloon under Trump. At the same time, consumer spending had at best a modest growth during Trump's term, so modest that economists ranked Trump twelfth from the bottom since the 1929 stock market crash.

The only fairly clear metric that Trump could rightfully point to in order to back his claim of great economic strength that was consistent during his four years was the stock market surge. The *Dow* did hover at or above historic highs. But again, much of that could be traced directly to low borrowing costs tied directly to record low interest rates. The low rates were already in place during Obama's second term. Also, there was no direct one-to-one correlation between a soaring stock market and economic strength.

The biggest flaw in Trump or any president taking credit for or getting blame for an up or down economy is that there are factors that no president can control. One is the fluctuation and manipulation of oil prices by the oil producers. Another is the continuing technological changes and innovations in society. And another is the impact of global financial and economic actions, natural disasters, and international conflicts.

*****

During his first term, Trump was obsessed with comparing his economic record with Obama's. It was always seemed like he had to top Obama and at the same time demolish him and his presidential legacy. His obsession was misspent and erroneous.

A cursory recapitulation of the economic numbers between Obama's second term and Trump's only term was stark proof of that. As previously mentioned, Trump's signature boast about the super high performance of the stock market in comparison to its performance during Obama's term proved nothing. The number of Americans that have any substantial stock ownership is tiny. The ups and downs of the market have no impact on their economic well-being.

There was another reason for the uptick in the market toward the end of Trump's term, and it was a politically embarrassing one for Trump. The market rose largely on the expectation of many investors for a Biden election victory and the Democrats recapturing the Senate. The widespread feeling was that this would be a boost for the economy, with Biden and the Democrats promising to spend trillions on green energy and infrastructure programs. That meant an even healthier stock market.

Trump's other signature economic boast was that his billions in corporate tax giveaways surged the economy. They didn't. The corporate beneficiaries did not rush out to spend the billions now in their pockets on job and business expansion. They used much of the tax largesse for stock buybacks, and hefty dividend payouts to big investors. This gave the illusion that the economy soared because of the tax cuts, as Trump endlessly claimed. It was good rhetoric, but it didn't hold up to the reality.

One economic measure that was a more reliable measure to use to compare Obama and Trump's economic performance was home purchases and sales. That metric directly affected the general public. Housing prices escalated during Obama's second term and continued to surge during Trump's term.

Then there was the debt. Trump's mammoth tax giveaways to corporations sharply reduced government revenue. That, together with Trump's big spending budget, escalated the country's debt burden. Trump said little about that for good reason.

The budget deficit during Trump's first three years, noted the Congressional Budget Office, was nearly one trillion dollars more than under Obama's last three years. The clear takeaways, then, in the Trump versus Obama economic performance comparison was that Trump did not best Obama hands down on the economy.

Trump benefited from the economic turnaround during Obama's second term, and no matter who sat in the Oval Office that person had marginal control at best over the shape of the economy. However, when things go bad, they get the blame. When they go well, they get the credit.

It was this crucial point that explained Trump's boasting about beating Obama's record. In truth, his record was Obama's record.

The best that could be said was that Trump would topple all barriers to corporate profit-taking and provide endless tax cuts and advantages to Wall Street and the major corporations in a second term. Then he would crow even louder every time an economic metric such as job growth or inflation were favorable even if, as would be the case, he benefited from his predecessor Biden's stewardship of the economy. During Biden's administration, joblessness hit even greater record lows than on Trump's watch.

Trump meanwhile would rip away or water down all regulatory rules for corporations and the financial industry as much as possible. At the same time, he'd give the oil and gas industry free rein to drill anywhere and everywhere on public lands. The rationale from him was always that these actions would surge the economy.

That would be an exact repeat of what he did or tried to do in his first term. The big winners again would be the rich. How much tens of millions of regular American workers and consumers would really gain from Trump's economic "miracle" plan would be anyone's guess.

11

Attacking the Sacred Cows: Medicare and Social Security

"Under no circumstances should Republicans vote to cut a single penny from Medicare or Social Security."
—Trump, from *Agenda 47*

In an interview with *CNBC* in March 2024, Trump seemed to give lie to his solemn pledge and admonition to the GOP to keep its hands off Medicare and Social Security. Here was the new Trump line: "There is a lot you can do in terms of entitlements, in terms of cutting and in terms of also the theft and the bad management of entitlements. There's tremendous amounts of things and numbers of things you can do."

So, which was it? Would Trump, once back in the Oval Office, hold Medicare and Social Security sacrosanct? Or would Trump, as many in the GOP have tried to do through the years, hack away at Social Security and Medicare? Trump, for the moment anyway, quickly recognized he had seemingly contradicted himself on how he'd deal with Medicare and Social Security in the *CNBC* interview and back-pedaled fast.

He told *Breitbart News*, "I will never do anything that will jeopardize or hurt Social Security or Medicare. We'll have to do it elsewhere. But we're not going to do anything to hurt them. There's so many things we can do. There's so much cutting and so much waste in so many other areas, but I'll never do anything to hurt Social Security."

Despite his vehement protests that he would not put a finger on Social Security or Medicare, Trump had two problems in trying to make his hands-off case. One was his presidential history. During his Oval Office tenure, his 2020 budget proposed slashes to Social Security and Medicare programs. If Trump's cuts had been enacted, tens of billions would have been cut from Medicare and Social Security programs and benefits.

Trump tried to put a palatable spin on it by claiming that there would be no direct cuts in the programs. The aim was solely to ferret out wasteful spending and provider payments, and to lower prescription drug costs. However, this was more than just accounting figure juggling.

The Federation of American Hospitals blasted Trump's proposed cuts as "devastating for seniors." The group pointed out the obvious. The heavy-handed slashes would leave recipients with fewer treatment options and the cost of treatment service would rise. There were also provisions for a work requirement and a repeal of Medicaid expansion. Both were tantamount to slashing programs and benefits.

As for Social Security, the Trump plan would have cut ten billion dollars from the Security Disability Insurance (SSDI) program. This program was designed to aid those with disabilities.

The cuts were not a "one and done" Trump budget proposal just for the 2020 budget. He made the same budget proposal cuts to Medicare and Social Security in every one of his four years in the White House.

*****

Trump had an even greater problem in selling his solemn pledge not to tamper with Medicare and Social Security—that was the GOP. Republicans had waged a long, relentless, unyielding war against Medicare and Social Security. Biden made pointed reference to that intense history and assault in his 2024 State of the Union Address, saying "Some Republicans want Medicare and Social Security to sunset every five years."

GOP leaders screamed in protest at Biden's words. But he was mostly right. The qualifier "mostly" is there only because it was more than just "some" Republicans that have taken dead aim through the years at gutting Medicare and Social Security. The first in the door was then-President Reagan. In May 1981, he unveiled a detailed plan for doing what had been unthinkable for nearly a half century—slashing Social Security.

The most draconian part of the Reagan plan was to sharply reduce the pensions of workers who retired before the age of 65, reduce payments to those who retired at the age of 65 and older, and completely abolish the limit on how much the elderly can earn without losing retirement benefits. Predictably, the plan drew angry howls from labor, senior advocacy groups, and Democrats. It went nowhere.

Reagan didn't give up. He tried three more times before the year was out. He wanted to cut benefits for all new retirees, which totaled three million people—90,000 of them women over age ninety. That also went nowhere.

He wanted to hack away at any increases for the then thirty-six million beneficiaries already receiving benefit checks. That also went nowhere. However, the groundwork was set for the GOP's sustained attack on Medicare and Social Security in the coming years.

In 2005, GOP president George W. Bush upped the ante. He lifted plans almost verbatim from the proposal concocted by the ultra-conservative Cato Institute after Reagan's failure to slash and burn Medicare and Social Security. That was branded the "Project on Social Security Privatization" and it would have allowed Social Security recipients to withdraw and invest part of their benefits into private accounts. That could be anything from stocks to conceivably even more risky speculative investments such as gold or silver. Predictably, it ignited a storm of protest and Bush backpedaled from the plan.

Meanwhile, Medicare faced its own GOP assault. The re-opening gun was the demand by then House Speaker Newt Gingrich that then President Clinton make big cuts in Medicare and Medicaid. Clinton did not.

The GOP, ever undaunted, found yet another way to put Medicare back on the chopping block when it took control of the House in 2010. This time the GOP demanded that Medicare recipients receive fixed sum vouchers that could be used to purchase private insurance. This would have effectively left millions of elderly recipients at the mercy of the private insurance market with no government back stop. The plan mercifully was a no-go.

However, ever relentless, the GOP found another way to hammer Medicare through the back door. GOP governors in more than a dozen states simply refused the federal government offer to expand Medicaid coverage in their states. They shunned the funds and funding. Millions of low-income seniors were in effect shut out of the system with no way to get health insurance, while the states that said "no" to coverage expansion rejected the billions the federal government had offered to bankroll their medical care.

*****

Based on the GOP's, and later Trump's, brutal history of trying to savage Medicare and Social Security, Biden was not far off the mark when he lambasted both for trying to hack away at the two popular entitlement programs. He also was smart to pledge that if he was re-elected, he would not only do everything to protect both programs from any tampering, he'd also propose measures to beef up both programs. Harris, as Biden's replacement as Trump's presidential opponent, almost certainly would make the same pledge.

This was a necessary pledge to make. For years, economists had warned that at some future date, usually set in the 2030s, both programs could run out of money. This was not merely partisan fearmongering. America's population was aging and that meant ballooning healthcare costs and Social Security benefit payments.

Biden's answer was to find more sources of revenue. Trump's answer did not go beyond his shaky promise not to touch both programs. However, given his and the GOP's long history of assault on Medicare and Social Security, characterizing his promise not to make cuts as "shaky" was being charitable.

12

Trump's War on Drugs

"We will not rest until we have ended the drug addiction crisis."
—Trump, from *Agenda 47*

Trump bolstered his big, bold, brash promise to finish the job in eradicating illegal drug use in the country by touting his alleged success as President in doing much to attain that goal. His claim that "we achieved the first reduction in overdose deaths in more than thirty years" would be impressive if indeed it was true.

Like so many of Trump's gargantuan boasts of success, this one was subject to much debate about just how true that really was. In fact, there was more falsity than fact to the claim. It was true that overdose drug deaths did drop in one year of his first term. The falsity was that this was the case for his entire four years.

During the other three years of his administration, the overdose death rate jumped, even hitting a record high in 2020, his last year in office. Trump's drug focus was almost exclusively on synthetic opioids, which were the hot ticket drug scourge in the nation's eyes—the overdose death rate for those jumped every year that Trump was in office.

Trump's vow, though, to win the drug war if re-elected had much more substance to it. He'd use the military, including the Navy, to bust up the drug cartels. He'd strong arm Mexico and other Latin American nations to crack down on drug smugglers. He'd permanently tag fentanyl as a federally-controlled substance. In line with that, he'd saber rattle China to knock off export of fentanyl's chemical precursors, or else.

He'd show maximum compassion toward addicts and their families with an array of jobs, counseling, and treatment programs to help them get and stay clean and sober. Then there was his spectacular and sensational vow that stirred the most chatter: he'd demand that Congress impose the death penalty on drug dealers and human traffickers.

He didn't distinguish between the small-time operators and the big murderous drug cartel dealers for who would be sentenced to death. Trump knew the eye-catching value of making this pledge. So much so that he made it the number one item on his detailed *Agenda 47* remake of America: "When I am back in the White House, the drug kingpins and vicious traffickers will never sleep soundly again. We did it once, and we did it better than anybody else."

But again, the death penalty? There were added problems that made this little more than a campaign sound bite bluster. One, federal law already had a capital punishment provision for major drug trafficking. Two, it was vague and hazy in that it must be shown that the traffickers actually caused the loss of human life. Third, applying the death penalty to drug traffickers almost certainly would be subject to legal and constitutional challenge.

"The court also has imposed other limitations: Even where a death does result from a felony but the defendant was not the actual killer, the defendant must additionally be (1) a major participant, and (2) exhibit reckless indifference to human life, in order to be eligible for capital punishment," noted *MSNBC* legal analyst Danny Cevallos. "Although federal drug crimes feature numerous mandatory minimum sentences, a mandatory death sentence would also likely be unconstitutional according to a 1976 Supreme Court case."

*****

In laying out his drug-combating agenda, as with every other agenda policy pledge, Trump took a round house shot at Biden. The checklist of Biden's alleged sins that surged the drug crisis per Trump was, of course, headed first and foremost by his accusation of a "let them all in" immigration policy. This supposedly opened the border wide to floods of drug dealers and traffickers, especially the cartels. Said Trump, "Hundreds of thousands of pounds of deadly drugs are now pouring across Biden's wide-open border and claiming the lives of over 100,000 Americans every year."

In addition to the alleged human cost, there was no surprise that he blamed that on Biden, too. Even more, he attributed the alleged staggering profits the big shot drug dealers made to Biden's supposedly porous to non-existent border policy. He placed the ill-gotten amount of profit they raked in at thirteen billion dollars.

There was no proof that any of this was true. However, by tying drugs to cartels and illegal immigration, Trump hit an emotional pitch that he knew would resonate with many Americans. The dangling questions that it didn't answer were how effective was Trump's war on drugs during his first term, and how effective would it really be in a second term?

A centerpiece of Trump's pledge to end the drug scourge that raised many eyebrows was his oft-stated call for the death penalty for cartel drug bosses—all for the most part a product of Biden's alleged open border immigration policy. There were two glaring problems with that. There was no evidence that the opioid crisis or any of the other illicit drugs were the sole product of drug cartel trafficking.

The other was that there was equally no evidence that, even if the death penalty were applied, it would curb trafficking. Not to mention the colossal moral and legal hurdles that trying to apply the death penalty in these extremely narrow instances would have to surmount.

During his term, Trump (minus the bit about the death penalty for cartel traffickers), did lay out a fairly comprehensive plan that put some emphasis on treatment and counseling. This was a more traditional, pro forma, and realistic approach to confronting the problem. That part of his plan was generally applauded by drug and medical treatment program advocates. Even then the Trump plan quickly returned to the heavy-handed law enforcement approach—tougher sentencing for even smaller amounts of drugs sold, an ironclad clamp down on the border, ports of entry, and the waterways supposedly to end smuggling.

*****

Yet once more, how effective was this approach to meeting Trump's goal of combating the scourge? Let's examine more closely Trump's claim that he repeated in 2023, three years after his term ended, that he marshalled the full power of his administration and achieved the greatest decline in drug overdose deaths in thirty years.

As mentioned before, drug overdose deaths did drop initially during Trump's term. But what he conveniently omitted from his victory lap was that by the end of his term, drug overdoses hit near record levels. That meant only one thing. There was more to cloud the picture of a drug war triumph. Drug deaths from the overuse of the synthetic opioid derivative fentanyl climbed higher every one of Trump's four years in office.

There was yet more to cloud the picture. A University of Pittsburgh research team that closely examined the drop in overdose deaths during the first year of Trump's term reported that the drop had less to do with Trump's tough measures and increased funding for treatment and law enforcement than with the availability of other opioid-related drugs.

The overdose deaths from those drugs remained constant. The researchers concluded, "The analysis we present here suggests an alternative explanation, that the decline in overdose deaths in 2018 was just a return to baseline exponential trajectory after a transient supply-side shock of highly potent illicit drugs."

That meant two things if true. One, many of the preventative measures Trump claimed he put into force during his first term failed to curb the problem. Two, the return to the same tough measures as before, including death penalties and border crackdowns, would do nothing to fulfill his boast that he would end the drug scourge in America.

Put bluntly, Trump would be yet another in the line of presidents that went back to Nixon who made lofty and soaring tough talk promises to wage and win the war on drugs. And just like them, he too would ultimately suffer the same inglorious defeat.

13

Trump's China Syndrome

"Biden's pro-China economic program puts America last and it's killing our country. My cutting-edge trade agenda will revitalize our economy by once again putting America first. We will quickly become a manufacturing powerhouse like the world has never seen before."
—Trump, from *Agenda 47*

Trump hit one of his biggest home runs during the 2016 presidential campaign when he thundered in campaign stop after campaign stop that he would bring major manufacturing industries back to America. This played well with many American workers, particularly in the Midwest, who had over the past two decades watched the mad dash of major American companies to Asia, Mexico, and other cheap labor and environmentally lax countries. Trump made the same pitch again for the 2024 presidential campaign.

This time around, though, there were some tweaks. The biggest was his threat that he'd slap punishing, crushing tariffs on foreign companies' imports to the U.S. Trump claimed that the big tariffs would "punish" foreign producers and "protect" American firms. He didn't stop there. He sharpened the threat by promising to impose even stiffer tariffs on companies that manipulated their currency and engaged in unfair trade practices.

He almost certainly had China in mind. Trump's economic war against foreign companies supposedly would create more jobs, lower inflation, and at the same time cut the costs of goods and services. That supposedly would save

American workers billions. The other sweetener was that it would sharply reduce America's trade deficit.

Trump capped this with the bellicose promise that his economic war with China would put a stop once and for all to China's buying up America. Said Trump, "We will also adopt new rules to stop U.S. companies from pouring investments into China, and to stop China from buying up America, allowing all of those investments that clearly serve American interests. We're not going to allow bad things to happen to our country anymore. And we will eliminate federal contracts for any company that outsources to China."

*****

The dangling questions in Trump's desired relaunch of the trade war, with the unabashed stated target of China, were did it work when he tried it during his term, and would it work with the added tough tweaks in a possible second term? The number one issue or, really, reason that Trump repeatedly insisted on the China trade war was that it would be a major boost to the economic well-being of American workers and consumers.

It wouldn't. In fact, it would do just the opposite. A study by the Peterson Institute for International Economics found that Trump's punitive tariffs would result, not in gaining billions in savings for Americans, but in Americans having to pay out a half billion dollars or more in price increases on imported goods.

That amounted to a staggering debt of nearly two percent of the nation's GDP. To fine-tune that even more, it would cost the average household almost two thousand dollars annually in raised consumer spending costs. Some analysts put the cost to the consumer even higher.

"This is the tip of the iceberg," said Kimberly Clausing, chair in tax law and policy at the UCLA School of Law. "The cost of retaliation will be very large. The Europeans will tariff us. The Mexicans and Canadians will be very upset. People aren't going to take it lying down."

Then there was the much-vaunted Trump claim that the punitive tariffs would create tens of thousands more jobs in this country. As with the claim of lower costs on products to consumers, the claim had no merit. A *Moody's* study placed the job loss, not gain, at a colossal 675,000 jobs. It further warned that inflation would jump, and the nation's GDP would drop.

That would almost certainly guarantee that the nation's economy would plunge into another recession, since other nations would retaliate with their own tariffs on American exported goods. That wasn't all. Trump's boast that the punitive tariffs would cut the nation's trade deficit didn't add up.

Maybe Trump forgot, but his trillion-dollar tax giveaway to the corporations and wealthy during his term was scheduled to expire in 2025. If he pushed to extend the tax cuts longer, as he vowed to do if re-elected, it would cost the nation an estimated four and half trillion in revenue lost.

As in all GOP tax cuts going back to Reagan in the 1980s, the big winners and gainers were the wealthy and corporations, not the tens of millions of American workers. They were the principal buyers of goods and services, not the super-rich. So, this would be a further drain on the economy, a revenue shift from workers to the rich, and an increase to the nation's deficit.

*****

There was more potential collateral damage in Trump's trade war. It would poison relations between nations, both friend and foe. That would complicate efforts by nations to cooperate on crucial issues such as immigration, combating terrorism, disease control, global warming, and the always thorny issue of nuclear weapons control.

Trump's trade war had one other nefarious consequence. It propagated the deeply held fiction that China or any other targeted nation would actually pay the tariffs that Trump would slap on them. They wouldn't pay a penny of the cost. American consumers would foot the bill. Corporations routinely pass on the added costs of raised tariffs to the consumer in the countries that hiked the tariffs.

It's a standard pass-on cost, or put another way, another cost of doing foreign business for a company. For every good that a punitive tariff dollar was tagged onto, the American buyer, not the Chinese exporter of its manufactured good would pay that extra dollar

"The 2018-2019 tariffs clearly raised consumer prices," Goldman Sachs economists noted in a report to clients in 2023, adding that these price increases were "borne almost entirely by U.S. businesses and households—not Chinese exporters."

Likewise, the U.S. International Trade Commission found in a 2023 study that U.S. importers "bore nearly the full cost" of tariffs. That independent agency estimated that prices increased by about one percent for each one percent increase in tariffs on Chinese-made goods, steel, and aluminum products.

Despite the economic pain that punitive tariffs would impose on American consumers, while doing nothing to punish China, Trump could potentially garner much political mileage from the threat of imposing them. It made it appear that he was talking tough and standing up to the Chinese and that he would not allow the U.S to be bullied by them.

This played well with millions who bought deeply into the myth that America had lost ground badly to China and other nations and the best way to regain that lost ground was to hit back against them. It was wrong-headed, counter-productive, and just plain damaging, but it sounded tough and even patriotic. And in a heated political battle with the highest stake of the road back to the White House on the line, that was good enough for Trump.

*****

There was one more disconcerting note sounded about just how much Trump really accomplished with his trade war. The note was sounded by Robert O'Brien, one of Trump's former national security advisors. Trump continually gave the impression that he had gotten China to back down and stop undercutting prices and volumes on American manufacturers' goods. Specifically, he bragged that he arm-twisted China into purchasing more than two hundred billion dollars of American goods.

He then took an extra victory lap on this by claiming that the deal ushered in a Nirvana in relations between the U.S.

and China: "One of the many great things about our just-signed giant Trade Deal with China is that it will bring both the USA & China closer together in so many other ways. Much more to come!" It didn't, because the deal Trump ballyhooed never happened. Trump, to no surprise, never uttered another word about China's reneging on the deal.

Though Trump would never admit failure, he did learn one lesson from China's saying no to the deal. That was to scrap his one-man go-it-alone bullying and get other nations to back him when he saber-rattled China again, if he got a second term. This time he'd try to enlist other nations to pressure China to alter its trade policies. He'd focus on one area of manufacturing that could hurt—that was China's growing dominance in the export of electric vehicles.

Trump calculated that it would be easier to get others on board to rein in China in this area of trade. China's alleged policy of dumping electric vehicles at low price hit other countries hard, too. On the surface, enlisting other nations in Trump's trade war appeared to be the wiser approach than the U.S. going it alone.

The big flaw in that, though, was that in a Trump second term he would not limit his punitive tariff to Chinese imports alone. His tariffs would be across the board; they would apply to friend and well as foe. So, in trying to nail China on electric vehicles, other foreign car makers would also be subject to Trump's punitive rates.

The only way to get around that would be to lower, not raise, the tariffs—which under a Trump trade war would be slapped on friendly nations as well as the Chinese. This would be particularly of those countries that were the most likely to go into partnership with the U.S. against China.

Yet that wasn't in the Trump tariff battle plan. One just had to harken back to Trump's own words on that score in 2018 at a NATO meeting on German car manufacturers: "See the millions of cars they are selling in the U.S. Terrible. We will stop this."

Now whether Trump would have been willing to reverse course on this view of potential ally Germany and try to woo them into a partnership against China's car exports was fanciful at best, and impossible at worst.

*****

Another major problem that Trump did not talk about or seemingly consider was that in any war there is more than one combatant. That combatant was the one that the war is being waged against. The enemy won't sit back and allow the opponent free rein to defeat them. They will fight back.

A trade war is no different. The entire history of nations that engaged in trade wars with other nations by slapping high-rate tariffs on their imports has shown one thing. The targeted countries retaliate by slapping high or higher tariffs on the other nation's manufactured products exports.

That was exactly what China did during Trump's first round of trade war tariffs in his first term. In some cases, the Chinese were forced to pay upwards of ten percent on the goods shipped into the U.S. What did they do? They turned right around and levied tariffs on U.S. goods shipped into China. And at times, these were double the tariffs imposed on their own goods.

The hardest hit were U.S. farmers in the South and Midwest. The USDA estimated that in 2018 and 2019 the U.S. paid out more than twenty-five billion dollars in tariff-related costs. It was not just the Chinese who imposed the tariff hikes. Canada and the European nations also imposed higher tariffs on U.S. imports. That swelled the costs and economic pain inflicted on U.S. farmers.

This was hardly the outcome Trump had in mind when he assured Americans that the tariff hikes would create more jobs. The exact opposite happened. Surveys showed the tariffs produced predictable job losses, not gains. Analysts soon coined a term that came to symbolize the grossly failed result of Trump's China trade war. The term was "China Shock." That referred to the big plunge in jobs that resulted from the increased tariffs on Chinese goods.

Researchers at Harvard's Kennedy School studied the impact of heightened tariffs extensively and were sharply critical of the effects of trade battles, issuing a detailed paper on the matter. "When you raise tariffs, there's no guarantee that you're going to reduce the value of imports; you might just increase prices instead. Once U.S. tariffs were in place, we saw U.S. firms expanding sales of goods that were competing with Chinese imports," observed economist Gordon Hanson, one of the paper's co-authors. "But the increase in sales was largely a result of higher prices and not greater quantities. The absence of a strong U.S. output response to tariffs on Chinese imports meant that the extra trade protection didn't translate into higher employment."

Trump, or at least the smarter heads around him, knew well that tariffs push prices up, hurt manufacturers and farmers, and certainly do not create more jobs. But Trump, and even Biden, still talked tough to China and promised to continue hitting them hard on the pricing of their goods imported into the U.S.

The reason for the strong-arm talk was simple. It played well with voters, especially GOP voters. Trump lambasting China for "stealing" or "controlling" America struck the right hard-nosed tone for many voters. The great irony is that those who were the most affected ("hurt" is probably the more accurate term) by the tariffs were the ones who cheered the loudest at Trump's trade war goad of the Chinese.

Many falsely equated higher prices with a Chinese flood of imports and just as falsely believed that this was part of a larger plot by the Chinese to take over American industry and control the country. It was nativism and xenophobia run amok. But the point was that it touched a deep nerve and to a large swatch of conservative voters it was just the right tonic to put America first again. It seemed to them to confirm Trump's Make America Great Again.

History provided ample proof that tariff wars plunged nations into economic misery, and a decade-long 1930s depression. They have been a major contributing factor to shooting wars and increased international tensions as well. However, it was good politics that played well for domestic consumption.

Trump understood that. That was why he would again make China America's trade Enemy Number One. But only this time around he intended to brag that he had won the war.

14

Boys Must Be Boys,
Girls Must Be Girls

"I will sign a new executive order instructing every federal agency to cease all programs that promote the concept of sex and gender transition at any age. I will then ask Congress to permanently stop federal taxpayer dollars from being used to promote or pay for these procedures and pass a law prohibiting child sexual mutilation in all 50 states. It'll go very quickly."
—Trump, from *Agenda 47*

Trump being ever attuned to any and every issue that caught fire as a divisive, controversial, but potentially vote-getting issue, it was inevitable that he'd latch onto one issue that fit that bill in every respect. Said he, "No serious country should be telling its children that they were born with the wrong gender—a concept that was never heard of in all of human history—nobody's ever heard of this, what's happening today. It was all when the radical left invented it just a few years ago."

By the start of the 2024 presidential campaign that issue was what and who was a male and female. A *Pew Survey* in June 2024 on "Gender identity, sexual orientation and the 2024 election," gave Trump plenty of ammunition. It found that most voters agreed that whether a person was a male or a female, their gender was assigned to them at birth. Among Trump supporters, the percent who agreed with that was even more lopsided. Ninety percent of Trump supporters agreed that genetic sex was assigned at birth.

Even more, the percentage of both GOP and Democratic voters leaped by more than ten percent in the period between Trump's first term and 2024. Black and Hispanic voters by a clear majority also agreed that the sex of an individual was identified at birth.

The *Pew Survey* decisively confirmed that there were millions of Americans debating, harping on, and enraged at the notion of genetic males transforming themselves into females or some variation of that and competing as women in sports and other competitive venues. Many were also put out that even small children might have their gender changed medically, surgically, or chemically.

Trump was among them and of course he blamed Biden for allegedly putting the federal government in the business of what had now been branded "gender affirming care."

Trump pledged to end all of that. He'd put a stop to any federal funding for any program that promotes transgenderism. He'd boot any hospital or clinic that performed sex gender procedures out of Medicaid and Medicare funding. He'd urge parents to sue doctors and hospitals that performed gender affirming procedures.

He'd weaponize the DOJ to go after any drug manufacturer and supplier that provided drugs for sex alterations. He'd weaponize the Education Department to crack down on teachers and administrators at schools that promoted gender transformation concepts.

He'd demand that schools exclusively teach and promote the traditional nuclear family as the only legitimate family-parent-child construct. He'd push Congress for a law that recognized only the standard genetic construct of male and female. He'd bring the full weight of his office to publicly cheerlead every effort to stop men from claiming transgenderism and competing in women's sports.

*****

If Trump got any traction for even one or two of these hard-nosed measures, the question, as with all of his other big, sweeping remakes of government in his image proposals, what would be the fall-out? The first result from any of Trump gender war actions would be that they'd generate mountains of fresh lawsuits from LGBTQ advocacy groups. Their suits would almost certainly wind up in courts that might or might not look with favor on a suit to block implementation of any of the Trump crusade's measures.

In June 2024, one district court dealt a blow to the push to expand gender affirming rights and protections. It temporarily blocked implementation of the Biden administration's new Title IX rule that expanded protections for LGBTQ+ students. It claimed that Biden overstepped the Education Department's authority.

This was just the opening legal assault on the issue. Seven other states also pushed in federal courts to block any further protections for LGBTQ+ students. On the flip side, LGBTQ+ advocates would almost certainly find judges in other sex discrimination cases that were sympathetic to their position.

In 2023 the ACLU and transgender advocacy groups filed more than a dozen cases that countered the anti-transgender health care bans. They filed more lawsuits against Trump's executive order banning transgender individuals from the military. In a few of the cases they scored wins. In others the cases remained pending after Trump left office. Still, it would be touch and go at best trying to win major victories against the transgender assault in the courts.

A 2024 report on the battle over transgender protections underscored that dilemma and danger, stating "Getting courts to understand the experience of transgender people and the impact of discriminatory policies on their lives was difficult even before Trump reshaped the judiciary. It was that much harder in the years after he was ousted from office. What was firmly established was that the courts were not as friendly as they once were."

*****

Trump would attack transgender protections through executive orders. Then, when the inevitable lawsuits were filed against them, a standard defense would be that to expand LGBTQ+ rights violated traditional religious rights and beliefs. Dragging religion into it would stir a firestorm on both sides of the issue. That would be just the kind of reaction a Trump administration would thrive on to stir up millions of religious conservatives.

The other weapon that Trump would have, and would not hesitate to wield, was the power of the purse. In his rants against transgender protections, he continually threatened anything and everyone, from doctors to hospitals to school districts, with the withholding of federal funding if they even hinted at doing anything that supported transgender medical procedures and rights protections. Whether Trump withholds funds or makes a push to get Congressional Republicans to block spending on all gender-affirming programs is less important than the climate of fear that the constant threat of defunding would pose.

Much would also depend on what the shape of Congress would be following the 2024 presidential election. A Trump win and a GOP-controlled House and or Senate would pose a towering obstacle that transgender advocacy groups would find tough to step around to ensure LGBTQ+ rights were protected.

Democrats had a slender majority in the Senate during Biden's term. They needed it to beat back the groundswell of new bills the House GOP introduced that threw up every kind of roadblock to transgender protections. With Trump in the White House saddle again, whether the GOP retook the Senate or not, the bills along with the executive orders would keep coming nonstop.

The other major battleground would be the states. Transgender advocacy groups would make a huge push in Democratic majority states such as California and New York to get state officials and state legislatures to strengthen their laws protecting transgender rights. They'd also push hard for officials in those states to provide greater funding for gender-affirming education and health care programs.

Trump and the GOP would of course vehemently oppose these efforts within the states. However, faced with what would be the solid wall of hostility from a Trump administration to transgender protections, or even transgender existence, LGBTQ+ advocates would need every ounce of support they could get from the courts, the states, and, hopefully, a Democratic-controlled House or Senate.

Though Trump would radically up the ante in the fight against transgender protections and even the existence of transgender persons, he is consistent if nothing else.

In the middle of his term, the Department of Health and Human Services circulated this draft memo, "Sex means a person's status as male, or female based on immutable biological traits identifiable by or before birth." The department proposed in the memo, which was drafted and circulated in the midpoint of Trump's term, that "The sex listed on a person's birth certificate, as originally issued, shall constitute definitive proof of a person's sex unless rebutted by reliable genetic evidence."

Sex could not and would not be changed; it was a biological, immutable condition that was determined. If that position had been adopted as iron-clad government policy that would have meant the end of any federal recognition of the million and half Americans who opted to declare themselves a gender other than their genetic sex at birth. "This takes a position that what the medical community understands about their patients—what people understand about themselves—is irrelevant because the government disagrees," noted Catherine E. Lhamon, who led the Education Department's Office for Civil Rights in the Obama administration and helped write transgender guidance.

Trump did not get to implement his anti-transgender assault because he was booted from office. He'd get another go at it a second time around and with public opinion on the issue mostly in his favor, the odds of him succeeding in a second term had soared.

15

"Black Jobs"

—Trump from *Agenda 47*

Trump's *Agenda 47* was stuffed with detail after detail on what he was going to do if he got another term. There was the military, inflation, the schools, energy, the environment, jobs, drugs, illegal immigration, law and order, trade, China, and much more. However, there was not a single word in his lengthy plan for America tract about race, more particularly African Americans and what special policies if any he'd put in place to deal with Blacks and racial injustice.

Whether by omission or commission, the glaring silence stood in sharp contrast to two things. In the June 2024 presidential debate with Biden, he pointedly referenced "Black jobs" and "Hispanic jobs" when the talk turned to the supposed disastrous impact illegal immigration had on fueling joblessness among Blacks and native-born Hispanics. Trump quickly tossed out the colossal number of eighteen to twenty million jobs that Blacks and Hispanics had allegedly lost.

The figure was fantastic, far-fetched, and grossly inaccurate. Black unemployment was at record lows. Black labor participation was at near record highs during Biden's term. The Bureau of Labor Statistics noted that overall unemployment among American-born workers was at near record lows.

Three months earlier in February 2024, the Economic Policy Institute report "Immigrants are not hurting U.S.-born workers," cited six facts to set the record straight about illegal immigrants and alleged job snatching from American workers: "It is clear the labor market is both absorbing immigrants and generating strong job opportunities for U.S.-born workers, including those in demographic groups potentially most impacted by immigration."

Not surprisingly, Trump's ludicrous assertion did not go unchallenged. "There is no such thing as a Black job. That misinformed characterization is a denial of the ubiquity of Black talent. We are doctors, lawyers, schoolteachers, police officers, and firefighters. The list goes on," noted Derrick Johnson, president and CEO of the NAACP. "A 'Black job' is an American job. It's concerning that a presidential candidate would seek to make a nonexistent distinction. But the divisive nature of this comment is not surprising for Donald Trump."

Things weren't so clear cut that Blacks uniformly denounced Trump on his claim that the flood of illegal immigrants were tossing countless numbers of Blacks in the unemployment line. There was division. Polls showed a mixed reaction.

A considerable number of Blacks did agree with Trump and blamed immigrants for taking jobs from them. An equally significant if not greater number of Blacks did not agree and saw no job loss to them from immigrants. The one thing that was clear was that Trump once again had found a sore nerve on an issue and would continue to exploit it.

He made the false charge about job-stealing immigrants in tandem with his other never-ending claim that his policies resulted in the lowest poverty rate ever among Blacks and Hispanics. "Last year (2019), Black and Hispanic American poverty reached the lowest ever in the history of our country." There was only partial truth in his claim and even the partial truth didn't tell the whole story. True, Black and Hispanic poverty rates were at a fifty-year low in his final year in office. The huge caveat was the perennial statistic that showed that Blacks and Hispanic poverty rates were always quantum leaps higher than whites.

The rosy picture Trump painted of new-found Black and Hispanic prosperity that he supposedly ushered in ignored the types of jobs that many Black workers were still relegated to: the bottom of the employment barrel, the lowest paying, with minimal health benefits and little security.

But there was still more to the prosperity nirvana for Blacks and Hispanics that Trump touted. That was, as noted earlier, that much of the economic recovery, job growth, and drop in poverty among Blacks and Hispanics came during the economic turnaround that began during Obama's second term. Poverty rates and joblessness had been steadily dropping then. Trump was the direct beneficiary of that turnaround. He inherited a growth economy. That growth made possible the upward economic climb of many Blacks and Hispanics.

*****

The other puzzling point about the silence in *Agenda 47* about African Americans and discrimination issues was that Trump had repeatedly boasted in 2020 and during the 2024 campaign that he did so much for Blacks. Trump's standard line, repeated everywhere on the campaign trail in the 2024, was, "I have done more for the African American community than any president with the exception of Abraham Lincoln."

It was a totally laughable quip that was roundly skewered by Trump foes and even some backers. Trump went into overdrive with this blatant falsity after the Floyd slaying in 2020. He again boasted that he'd done so much to improve the lives of Blacks. He conveniently said nothing about the systemic racial attitudes and practices endemic in some police departments that led to the killing and brutalization of many Blacks.

However, he did take a small victory lap on this issue by once more citing his very dubious dedication to criminal justice reforms: "We signed a landmark criminal justice reform bill that nobody thought was possible to think about. I did that. I did that. I got that done."

Dubious is being charitable in labeling Trump's action some kind of grand step forward on criminal justice reform. His signature accomplishment in this arena was his much touted First Step Act, signed in December 2018.

Under the Act's provisions, several thousand low-level petty offenders were released from federal prisons, a disproportionate number of which were Blacks and Hispanics. This was supposedly a major step toward slashing the bloated number of persons warehoused in America's jails and prisons, a number that annually made America the leading incarcerator in the world by far.

Trump's claim to be the great criminal justice reformer unraveled fast. His Justice Department put up endless barriers to releasing many of those eligible for early releasee. In more than a few cases, the department tried to reincarcerate those released, and tried to put a freeze on new release applications. "The law may let thousands of federal inmates out early," noted Stanford University drug policy expert Keith Humphreys, "but more than 1700 persons are released from prison every day already—so the First Step Act in one sense only equated to adding a few more days of typical releases to the year."

Trump worked hard to give the impression that the Act was his brainchild. It wasn't. Various proposals and actions on sentencing reform had been worked through over time by the Clinton and Obama administrations, in line with Congress. The reform plans extended back two decades before Trump came along. He simply took credit for those earlier substantive efforts.

Even more, whatever appearance Trump tried to make as premier criminal justice reformer he more than undid that with his bellicose, borderline racist slam of Back Lives Matter (BLM) protests. He escalated the attacks by repeatedly threatening to send in the National Guard and even the military to quell protests against police abuse in some cities.

He called BLM and the protests "a symbol of hate." He never missed a chance to tout the police, demand more of them, and on occasion slipped into raw thuggery by appearing to condone police violence and advocating taking the wraps off the use of the racist-tinged stop-and-frisk policing.

*****

One of Trump's signature lines during the 2016 presidential campaign, which he never tired of shouting, was, "What the hell do you have to lose?" His point was that the Democrats supposedly had taken the Black vote for granted, because Blacks loyally delivered that vote to them, election after election. Yet, they got little in return for that loyalty from the Democratic Party.

In 2024, he repeated variations on that pitch to Blacks again. This time there seemed to be a difference in some of the polls. At times they showed that more Blacks than ever were enthused about putting him back in the Oval Office.

He added a special sweetener to this in a two-hour speech before a Black political conservative group in South Carolina in February 2024, just before the GOP primary there. "Some of the greatest evils in our nation's history have come from corrupt systems that try to target and subjugate others to deny them their freedom and to deny them their rights," Trump said. "I think that's why the Black people are so much on my side now because they see what's happening to me happens to them." He not only claimed that he had done more for Blacks than most other presidents, now he claimed that he was victimized by an unjust criminal system like so many Blacks.

Political pundits, commentators, analysts, and Democratic party officials had a field day laughing at, ridiculing, and mocking Trump's braggadocio boast that Blacks adored, identified with, and even loved him. He claimed that legions of Blacks walked around with t-shirts on with a picture of his infamous mug shot of him being booked in Georgia after being charged with vote tampering.

One could skip past Trump's usual overblown self-promoting gaslighting. However, what couldn't be so mockingly dismissed was the polls that showed that more

Blacks than ever did say they backed Trump. The uptick in support among Blacks for Trump from various polls ranged from ten to twenty percent higher than in his 2020 presidential run.

The polls also showed a sharp generational divide. Blacks aged fifty and older were far more likely to back Biden than younger Blacks aged eighteen to forty-nine. CNN political data analyst Harry Enten was partially in shock from the jump in Black support for Trump. He warned, " "If this continued into November, Trump could win a larger share of Black voters than any Republican candidate since 1960.

He further warned, "This is historic. This is what a lot of folks have been talking about, that Joe Biden has a specific problem among younger Black voters, and that is exactly what is showing up right here. It's these younger Black voters who very much are turning on him and being much more supportive of Donald Trump than they were four years ago."

There was good reason to believe that more Blacks leaned toward supporting Trump in 2024. There was even more reason to worry about this deeply troubling possibility. However, with Biden's withdrawal from the race in July 2024, Biden's replacement Harris immediately energized many Blacks, especially Black women who donated tens of millions to her campaign. That quickly changed the racial equation against Trump.

In his presidential victory in 2016 and loss in 2020, he did marginally better with Black voters than prior GOP presidential candidates. That alone was not much cause for concern, let alone cause to get out the worry beads that

Trump and the GOP had made any kind of real breakthrough in prying Blacks aways from the Democrats.

Despite all the supposed grousing among Blacks about Biden, even before he dropped out, he did even better with Black voters in the bellweather South Carolina primary in January than he did in 2020. There was no break in the solid Democratic ranks by Blacks. That pattern was duplicated in other crucial primary elections in 2024.

Focus groups of Black voters confirmed that while more than a few Blacks continued to voice criticism and concern about some of Biden's policies, and even dredged up his enthusiastic support of the punitive Clinton Crime Bill in the mid-1990s, almost none said they had any love, like of, or desire to throw their lot in with Trump.

*****

Yet, the harsh reality was that thousands of Blacks did vote for Trump in 2020. Their reasons were easy to explain. Trump touched a tiny nerve with his shout that poor, underserved Black neighborhoods were supposedly a mess with lousy public schools, high crime and violence, and chronic joblessness and poverty.

He dumped the blame for that squarely on the Democrats who have run most of these cities for decades. Trump doubled down on that slam with a handful of carefully choreographed appearances with high-profile Black preachers at name Black churches. This was just enough, for some Blacks, to take the hard and sharp edge off the almost-set-in-stone image of Trump as a guy with a white sheet under his suit.

There was more. As far back as the 2004 presidential election, there was a sign that more than a few Blacks, most notably Black conservative evangelicals, were deeply susceptible to GOP conservative pitches on some issues. A considerable number of them voted for Bush that year and that was enough to give him the cushion he needed to bag Ohio and win the White House.

The same polls during that election that showed that Blacks' prime concern was with bread-and-butter issues—and that Bush's rival, Democrat rival John Kerry, was viewed as the candidate who could deliver on those issues—also revealed that a sizable number of Blacks ranked abortion, gay marriage, and school prayer as priority issues. Their concern for these issues didn't come anywhere close to that of white evangelicals, but it was still higher than that of the general voting public.

In 2008 and 2012, Black GOP advocacy groups ran ads hammering the Democrats again for their alleged indifference to, and outright aiding and abetting of, Black suffering in the inner cities, and touting the GOP's emphasis on small business, school choice, and family values as the best path to black advancement. This pitch always had some appeal to many Blacks. And though it would never trigger any kind of stampede to the GOP by even most of these conservative-leaning Blacks, it was enough to take some of the sting out of the GOP's naked history of racial abuse.

*****

Trump understood enough of that history. He tailored the few pitches he made to Blacks for their votes to reflect the stock GOP pro-business, free enterprise, and the healthy economy line as something that Blacks also could, and should, embrace. He used the same template in 2024 with the added twist that he was supposedly a victim of a horribly racially skewed criminal justice system just as Blacks are. The ten-to-twelve percent of Blacks who voted for Trump in 2016 and 2020, combined with the numbers who didn't vote at all, or didn't vote for Clinton or Biden, did not help elect Trump. He won with an Obama-like crusade among less-educated white male and female, blue collar, and rural voters. However, enough Blacks did buy his pitch that a conservative Republican businessman, with a horrifically tainted racial history, was a better bet in the Oval Office than a Democrat. This again made Trump's 2024 pitch to Blacks even more fraught with peril, even with Harris replacing Biden.

16

Smashing the Deep State

"I will shatter the Deep State and restore government that is controlled by the People."
—Trump, from *Agenda 47*

The one item in Trump's out-sized remake of America agenda that by far got most puzzled, nervous, and angered attention was his vow to "shatter the Deep State." The use of the term sounded like a page straight out of some New Order conspiratorial playbook.

There was no far out, kooky conspiracy reading in Trump's vow, nor in his characterization of "the Deep State." Put simply, the Deep State in Trump's view was for all intents and purposes the entire federal government. He was precise about what he'd do about it. He'd fire anyone he considered a "rogue bureaucrat." That meant liberals, leftists, whistleblowers, and anyone who even remotely disagreed with his policies.

He'd rid the National Security and intelligence gathering agencies of employees who he claimed "persecuted"—that is, who conducted investigations of the activities of anyone not a leftist radical. He'd overhaul the Foreign Intelligence Surveillance Act (FISA) with special emphasis on who the targets of surveillance are. He'd appoint a Truth and Reconciliation Commission to open to public view all documents on government spying. He'd aggressively monitor, audit, and downsize all intelligence agency spying operations.

He'd decentralize the federal government by moving agencies and departments all over the country—anyplace but the Capitol. This was his boldest, most innovative way to prove that he really meant to "drain the swamp" of leftist government hacks, bureaucrats, and obstructionists. Trump also had his eye on Congress. It figured heavily in his drain the swamp assault. He'd back a constitutional amendment to impose term limits on congressional representatives.

Trump critics immediately piled on and branded the plan overblown, bombastic, vindictive, and dictatorial. But most damning, they called it a colossal prescription for governmental disaster. Trump backers and the ultra-conservative Heritage Foundation fired back. They called it a much needed, government saving plan that by dismantling bureaucracy would exorcise the corruption, mismanagement, and most importantly liberal and even left-wing dominance that they claimed tainted the federal government. Though the plan's proponents and critics were at polar opposite ends, they agreed that if any part of the plan ever came into being it would confer tremendous power over all areas of government decision-making into Trump's hands.

Trump would accomplish power seizure in three ways. The first would be to strip nearly all employees of civil service protection. That would destroy the system that since the nineteenth century had insulated federal employees from being hired or fired at the personal and political whims of a president. Without that protection they'd serve at the president's pleasure. They'd be little more than "yes" men and women, carrying out without question the president's dictates.

The exodus of experienced, professional, and knowledgeable agency employees from the departments would be a flood. The same would apply to the agencies they worked for. They'd be government agencies in name only. Trump would have ironclad control over them.

Their independence and decision-making power would be totally removed. "Almost all Western democracies have a professional civil service that does not answer to whatever political party happens to be in power, but is immune from those sorts of partisan wranglings," noted Kenneth Baer, a former senior OMB official under President Obama. "They bring a technical expertise, a sense of long history and perspective to the work that the government needs to do. Making thousands of additional positions subject to political change risks losing that expertise, while bringing in people who are getting jobs just because they did some favor to the party, or the president was elected. And so, there's a risk of corruption."

*****

The second way Trump's Deep State break-up would put the power of the throne in his hands would be through his radical decentralization of governmental departments. He'd do it in two ways. One would be to drastically downsize and even eliminate some departments. This plan has been on the ultra-conservative drawing board for years.

Their special targets are the Department of Homeland Security, the FBI, the Environmental Protection Agency, and the departments of Education and Commerce. At the same time, they'd reduce commissions such as the Federal Communications Commission and the Federal Trade

Commission to nothing more than mouthpieces for Trump and the right.

The second way would be to move the administrative headquarters of government agencies from Washington D.C. to distant places throughout the country. The places that Trump had in mind almost certainly wouldn't be in reliable blue states, such as Democrat top-heavy states like California and New York, but to conservative states and towns. Grand Junction, Colorado, was a concrete example of that. During his term he moved the head office of the Bureau of Land Management (BLM) there in 2019. Trump made clear that the real motive behind the location move was that he wanted to assure government agencies were staffed and run in "places filled with patriots who love America." He got his wish, with the predictable stampede of employees who resigned from the agency rather than relocate.

"The vast bulk of (headquarters) employees left the agencies," observed Max Stier, president and chief executive of the Partnership for Public Service, a nonpartisan group that promotes serving in government. "It led to the loss of expertise that had been built up over decades," he said. "It destroyed the agencies."

Black and Hispanic employees made up a disproportionate number of those who left the BLM. Predictably, diversity within the BLM plunged. The same would happen again but on a far more massive scale if Trump moved most if not all the government agencies during a second term to far-away locations where the only employees would be "patriots who love America. And they really do love America."

*****

The third way Trump would accomplish his goal of putting the federal government totally in his hands would be to corral the intelligence-gathering agencies. Target number one would be a total overhaul of the Foreign Intelligence Surveillance Act (FISA). Said Trump, "We will totally reform FISA courts which are so corrupt that the judges seemingly do not care when they are lied to in warrant applications. So many judges have seen so many applications that they know were wrong, or at least they must have known. They do nothing about it, they're lied to."

The courts that he called lying and corrupt are charged with the review and approval of government wiretapping requests. The courts took much heat from Trump and rightists on one side, and from liberals and civil liberties groups on the other. The criticism was that they routinely rubber stamp nearly all government requests for the surveillance and wiretapping of U.S. citizens, without question or real oversight.

Trump rightly noted that this led to potential and real civil liberties abuses and infringements. Or, even less charitably, the harassment of Americans. Many of them posed no threat. They were tracked only because of their left, or more importantly for Trump, their hard-right political views.

His demand that a Truth and Reconciliation Commission be set up was his way of striking back at the courts and the intelligence agencies. On the surface, it looked to be a fair and open process that would give the public an unheard-of window into the deliberately opaque and secretive operations of intelligence agencies. Trump insisted that by opening the agencies up to public viewing this would end illicit government spying, censorship, and corruption.

The commission proposal was the least likely to ever happen, since government surveillance is the established bread and butter of the U.S. government's efforts to combat real and manufactured terror threats to the country. The real aim was not public disclosure of surveillance activities but rather that Trump's political allies, cronies, and any personnel connected to or doing Trump's bidding would not be the targets of surveillance and intelligence. Their targets should exclusively be Trump enemies.

The other proposals would all tie back in to the main Trump aim for the federal government—total control. The crackdown on government whistleblowers would silence any critic of Trump dictates within government. They'd be faced with stiff prison sentences if they spoke out. He made that clear in a 2018 tweet. He called leakers "traitors and cowards." His demand for an independent audit of all intelligence agencies on the surface seemed like a reasonable reform. "I will ask Congress to establish an independent auditing system to continually monitor our intelligence agencies to ensure they are not spying on our citizens."

That gave the noble appearance that Trump wanted greater government accountability and his sole aim was to protect citizens from illicit and intrusive government snooping. It was no such thing. He quickly added, "Or that they are not spying on someone's campaign like they spied on my campaign."

Trump's real motive then was to ensure that intelligence agencies kept hands off any of his personal or political actions and those connected with them.

The only arguably populist part of his "smash the Deep State" plan was to slap term limits on Congress. That had been proposed on various occasions by government accountability watchdog groups. Polls showed that a significant percentage of Americans favored term limits. At the same time, many GOP and Democratic congressional leaders also had voted on proposals to apply term limits to congresspersons. Predictably, the proposals died a fast death. Trump's revival of the proposal had the requisite populist flavor to it when he solemnly declared that his term limit plan would "shatter the deep state and restore government that is controlled by the people and for the people."

There was far less than met the eye in Trump's term limit call. He well knew that it would take passage and ratifying a constitutional amendment for enactment. That was a near impossibly high mountain to climb. It would require a two-thirds majority in the House and Senate and ratification from at least thirty-eight states. This would almost certainly be one among others in his Deep State attack that would be forgotten or wither on the political vine.

That was less important than, as with the plan itself, proving that Trump again would be a president who was a true champion and protector of the people against an alleged oppressive, intrusive, leftist-dominated federal government. The Deep State take-down then, as Trump presented it, was not a personal grab for total power and control but a heartfelt, genuine effort to put American "patriots" back in control.

17

Remaking America—
PROJECT 2025

In late June 2024, a Trump campaign spokesperson issued this statement: "None of these groups or individuals speak for President Trump or his campaign... Policy recommendations from external allies are just that—recommendations."

The Trump camp issued that statement to quell the sudden burst of media and public furor over the ultra-conservative Heritage Foundation's *Project 2025*. The project was a big, full blown, radical rightist nine-hundred-plus page blueprint for remaking the federal government and, by extension, America.

Trump evidently was not satisfied with the matter-of-fact denial. He quickly posted on his social media site, "I know nothing about *Project 2025*. I have no idea who is behind it." Whether Trump was deliberately lying or had a memory lapse, it strained credulity to the limit to believe his denial. It had been kicking around publicly for more than year before Trump claimed ignorance of it.

The Heritage Foundation released it in April 2023 with much fanfare on the right. Many of those who were or had been an intimate part of Trump's political brain trust were charter members of the Heritage Foundation. They had a direct hand in crafting the blueprint.

One of the principal crafters was Russ Vought, Trump's Office of Management and Budget director. Members of Trump's PAC-funded groups also sat on the project's advisory board, including the Conservative Partnership Institute, an organization led by Trump's former White House Chief of Staff Mark Meadows, which received a one-million-dollar donation from Trump's Save America PAC in 2021. There was a slew of other names cited who had been key parts of Team Trump during his term. To be exact:

—Six former cabinet secretaries

—Four persons nominated for ambassadorships

—First Deputy Chief of Staff

—A Former Chief of Staff

—Several leading Trump attorneys

—Over one hundred other former Trump officials

*****

It didn't require a close read of *Agenda 47*, Trump's sweeping template for a radical right remake of the country, to see that with few exceptions, *Project 2025* and *Agenda 47* were almost identical in what they proposed for the nation. As one example, in *Agenda 47* Trump laid out his planned assault on the Deep State which entailed slashing or outright eliminating such federal agencies as the Education Department, the Commerce Department, the EPA, the Department of the Interior, and the Food and Drug Administration.

He went into great ideological detail to tell why they must be whittled down or entirely eliminated. *Project 2025* made the same call for slashing or eliminating these agencies. It also went into great ideological detail to tell why. It used much of the same language and same reasoning in telling why.

It was true that think tanks of all political stripes, be they progressive, liberal, right, and ultra-right, or independent, continually make recommendations for reform on all policy issues. Some of the proposals eventually wind up as changes in agency operations, legislation, or presidential executive orders to implement. However, *Project 2025* was far different again because of the intimate tie between Trump and the Heritage Foundation. In fact, so intimate and so confident of the symbiotic connection with Trump that its complete formal title was the "2025 Presidential Transition Project."

✳✳✳✳✳

What then was that language and the reasoning behind the Heritage Foundation's overhaul of the government that Trump, despite denials, in some places lifted almost verbatim from? As already mentioned, there were two centerpieces of *Project 2025* and *Agenda 47*. The first would give Trump total control of all federal government agencies. He could hire and fire at will. The hires would serve purely at his pleasure. The agencies would be forbidden to take any independent action, particularly on regulations, without Trump approval.

Key regulatory agencies such as the EPA would either be eliminated or pared down. Trump's nemesis the Department of Justice and the FBI would be transformed into Trump's personal legal hit force to hector, harass, and prosecute political foes, mainly liberal and leftist critics.

The second key component of *Project 2025* and *Agenda 47* was the issue that was near and dear to the hearts and fury of ultra-conservatives, the battle over traditional family values. The battle began with the SCOTUS decision Roe v. Wade on abortion in the 1970s, intensified with the fight over legalizing gay marriage four decades later, and Obama and Biden administrations' executive orders strengthening transgender identity protections. The two documents made it clear that the federal government should seek to "maintain a biblically based, social science-reinforced definition of marriage and family."

There was still more proof that Trump or at least key Trump presidential campaign personnel were thoroughly versed on *Project 2025*'s aims. As early as January 2023, Spencer Chretien, Associate Director of the 2025 Presidential Transition Project at the Heritage Foundation, gave a detailed glimpse of *Project 2025*'s objectives in an op-ed in the *American Conservative*, widely read on the right.

He positioned *Project 2025* as a directive to Trump to craft an administration "more friendly to the right." He made the same claim that Trump repeatedly made, namely that the left through its alleged "vast power" had taken over "American institutions" and it was time for conservatives to take them back.

The well-worn and well-organized rightist action plan for the remake of government, as he explained, was the handiwork of several dozen right-wing organizations and hundreds of conservative activists and scholars. The action plan rested on four major pillars.

The first was the policy book *Mandate for Leadership*. It laid out exactly how ultra-conservatives would redefine the role of government agencies and ensure that Trump would move quickly to do the overhaul.

The second pillar left nothing to chance. It was the compilation in an online database of the names of "rock-solid conservatives" who could and would be selected to fill positions in the Trump administration. These were individuals who would faithfully carry out *Project 2025*'s stated goals.

The third pillar was something cleverly innovative—a Presidential Administration Academy. The idea here was to not only stuff an incoming Trump administration with "rock solid conservatives," but to ensure that they hit the ground running. The Academy would make the appointees and staffers "into experts in governmental effectiveness." This was crucial for them to avoid being blind-sided, tripped up, and stymied by the alleged liberal and leftist bureaucrats who knew all the ins and out of government rules and technicalities and could toss endless roadblocks in the way.

The fourth pillar was the true end game. That was to translate the lofty ultra-conservative wish list of objectives into public policy in every government agency. *Project 2025* aimed to leave nothing to chance in its planned government takeover and remake.

The Heritage Foundation would not make the mistake that it felt conservatives had made during Trump's term in 2016. They failed to quickly take advantage of the opportunity they had to totally overhaul the shape of the federal government in the ultra-conservative image.

By the time conservatives were able to figure out how to accomplish that, it was too late. Trump was ousted from office. *Project 2025* both warned and promised, "The usual suspects in the permanent political class will be ready for the next conservative administration. Will we be ready for them?" That's where *Project 2025* comes in."

There was one further item about Trump and *Project 2025* that did not go unnoticed. A few days after Trump vehemently denied any knowledge of *Project 2025* or any connection to him, a recruitment video for *Project 2025* appeared on Trump's *Truth Social* social media platform which featured a Trump campaign spokeswoman. There was no report that Trump denied authorizing it, or immediately took it down, or that it got there purely by accident or coincidence. So much for Trump denials.

18

"This is Not a Gun Problem"

Gun Control
"..."
—Trump from *Agenda 47*

"**E**very single Biden attack on gun owners and manufacturers will be terminated my very first week back in office, perhaps my first day,"

There were two towering ironies in Trump's defiant pledge to undo any and every restriction on gun ownership. The first was where he made the bellicose pledge. He made it at a campaign rally in Pennsylvania in early 2024.

The second, even greater irony is that barely five months after he shouted that he'd have no truck with restrictions on guns, he was the victim of gun violence in an assassination attempt on him in July 2024 at a campaign rally in, of all places, Pennsylvania.

The gun that shooter Thomas Matthew Crooks used in the apparent effort to kill Trump appeared to have been legally purchased. In addition, he had a small arsenal in his home. Whether these weapons were legally purchased or not, the fact that he was able to stockpile an arsenal with little notice or scrutiny underscored the deep peril of unrestricted access to guns.

There was much speculation in the aftermath of the Trump shooting that the debate over gun violence and gun control measures would now move front and center in the presidential campaign. There was even more speculation over whether Trump would soften his hardline stance on opposing tougher gun control restrictions.

One hint at the answer to that was Trump's *Agenda 47* and what it said about gun control, or rather what it didn't say about it. There was not a single word in the verbose Trump agenda to remake America on gun control or even gun violence. His silence on this crucial issue was even more deafening when he waxed at length on nearly every other policy issue in his radical program for government change.

Trump reset his long-standing template for dealing with any and every effort to rein in gun proliferation in a keynote address to an NRA confab in April 2023. He minced no words on guns: "I was proud to be the most pro-gun, pro-Second Amendment president you've ever had in the White House."

The hard-nosed NRA gun audience went berserk. They leapt to their feet, shouting and chanting "USA, USA." There was not the slightest indication that the mass shootings that had just happened in Tennessee and Kentucky, claiming many lives, had registered even a blip on Trump's or the NRA's awareness.

If anything, the inevitable calls for tougher gun control measures after a mass shooting spurred on the NRA and anti-gun control advocates, and that included Trump at the lead, to dig in their heels even more defiantly in saying an absolute "no" to any proposal to rein in gun ownership in America. The convention underscored the gun mania of both the NRA and Trump. There were massive displays in the exhibit hall of every type of gun and gun accessory imaginable.

Trump didn't stop with the obligatory rhetorical cheerleading of virtually unrestricted gun ownership. He also had a goody bag of gifts that he would dole out if re-elected president to strengthen gun ownership. Those included demanding that Congress pass legislation allowing the carrying of concealed weapons in all states, and tax credits to subsidize gun purchases and training for teachers. He also reminded the gun crowd that he made sure his picks to the SCOTUS were staunch anti-gun control advocates. He'd do the same with future court picks.

*****

However, as Trump well knew, the name of the game in thwarting all meaningful gun control measures was the National Rifle Association. The NRA's dominance was almost untouchable. Nowhere was that more evident than in the organization's relationship with Congress.

Contrary to the public perception and the political criticisms of the NRA and Congress, congressional Republicans were never the only culprits that stymied all impactful gun control legislation. More than a few Democrats also had been staunch opponents of gun control measures. Dozens of them through the years had taken tens of thousands in campaign cash from the NRA.

The NRA has been wildly successful in keeping its Republican and Democratic backers in the fold through a well-oiled, well-versed labyrinth of PACs, lobbyists, legal counsels, divisions, funds, and a foundation. The NRA has these divisions: Federal Affairs, Public Affairs, Finance, Research & Information, Conservation, Wildlife & Natural Resources and, most importantly, the NRA Political

Victory Fund. Its scorecard of wins was nothing short of phenomenal.

In 2008 it was directly or indirectly involved in nearly three hundred campaigns for the House and Senate. NRA-backed candidates or incumbents won two hundred and thirty of them. It spared little expense in padding its congressional win scorecard.

It ranked in the top tier of contributions received, lobbying dollars spent, and money garnered and spent by its PACs. But it was not just the NRA's money and willingness to spend it to pack Congress with pro-gun backers. It also cherry-picked former government officials or job-holders to do its congressional arm-twisting for it. Many of its lobbyists had government ties.

The assumption that the NRA was basically a front for conservative GOP business and political interests was another bad misread. Though a big share of the NRA's campaign dollars went to Republicans it was adept at spreading the largess around. Democrats over the years received several million in NRA campaign contributions.

The NRA got a stupendous return on the millions it spent on federal elections. Following the expiration of the ban on assault weapons in 2004, many gun control bills died stillborn in House and Senate committees.

There was little movement in the states to get tougher gun control laws. A majority of the states at the time of the 2024 presidential election still had minimal gun checks, while others had only slightly more restrictive controls on guns.

The Sandy Hook massacre in 2012 plopped the NRA on the nation's hot seat. The White House, many lawmakers, and much of the public demanded that the NRA soften its inflexible opposition to any gun control measures. That might have done much to stem the public clamor for stronger measures on storage of weapons, and tighter screening and background checks, maybe even borrowing a page from the tobacco industry's PR gambit and advocating for hazard warnings on the improper use of guns, or even offering to be part of a national conversation on gun violence.

That didn't happen. And with the election of Trump in 2016, the chance of getting any White House backing for full-blown bans on the big-ticket deadly weapons was nil. Trump and the NRA by then had the coziest of cozy relations.

Any kind of gun control advocacy would also have jeopardized the near bottomless storehouse of funding that the organization has received from gun industry interests and supporters. It would instantly turn off thousands of avid gun owners that look to the NRA to be its political mouthpiece in Washington and in the states for unfettered gun rights. Trump certainly understood that.

After each fresh mass bloodletting, a majority of Americans screamed loudly for Congress to do something, anything, to stop the gun carnage. The NRA was always singled out as the group with the blood on its organization's hands.

Trump did not see it that way during his term. He made it even clearer that he would not see it that way again if re-elected. Even when the blood spilled as a result of gun violence was Trump's, that still did not change things when it came to Trump doing anything to rein in gun violence in America. America would remain, courtesy of Trump and the NRA, as it always managed to be—a modern day wild, wild West.

Conclusion

"Our populist movement to Make America Great Again is the only force on earth that will lead our country back to safety, prosperity, and peace. I will never stop fighting for you, the American People, against the failed political establishment."
—Trump, from *Agenda 47*

Former President Donald Trump, as only Trump could do, boldly, brashly, brazenly, and most importantly supremely confident in himself, made the promise to again rescue America in the mission statement of his public policy manifesto, *Agenda 47*. The two operative words in his mission statement were "again "and "great."

Trump vowed throughout *Agenda 47* and in virtually every interview, speech, and talk he gave, to finish the job he started during his one term. The "great" part was his big, sweeping, no-holds-barred program to remake America in the most radical political blend of hardcore right and populist ideology that had come down the pike in American political history.

He had as his perennial foil—first, Democratic opponent President Joe Biden. When Biden exited the race, Trump pirouetted quickly to his replacement, Kamala Harris. He had a wealth of issues to pick, prod, and hammer at and on during the 2024 presidential campaign.

Through much of the campaign, one of them—illegal immigration— loomed at or near the top of the nation's worry list in 2024. Trump didn't stop at simply promising to roll back Biden's executive orders which sought to balance tighter border control with protecting the rights of immigrants.

Trump vowed to mass deport every illegal immigrant alleged or accused of any crime, to pump billions more into border enforcement, and to use every federal law enforcement agency to stop the flow of illegal immigrants. He topped this by reiterating his controversial scheme to try to seal off the entire border with a wall.

He wasn't finished and in his *Agenda 47*, he tacked on an even more draconian measure if re-elected: "I will stop the outrageous abuse of parole authority. I will reinstate my action making illegals ineligible for public housing. We will terminate all work permits for illegal aliens. And I will demand that Congress send me a bill blocking any future President from abusing his power to distribute welfare benefits in this manner. It's all being paid for by the American taxpayer." No president in American history had ever gone that far. But now Trump had.

Trump cast an ever-wider net by tossing in Hamas. He claimed that every one of their supporters in the U.S. was tantamount to an embedded dangerous foreign alien. He'd hunt down every supposed Hamas supporter on every college campus and hustle them out of the country.

In line with that, he'd quickly put back in place what he called his "wonderful" travel ban on "radical Islamic terrorists." That, in effect, again would mean banning any Muslim from coming into the country.

*****

Trump's markedly blunt style and boasts were radically different from Biden's approach to policy in another big way. Biden's proposals on crucial issues were fleshed out, thoughtful, and detailed. Trumps were sledgehammer swipes at policy decisions.

He'd do away with the Department of Education and let the states and parents handle all matters about education policies and practices at all levels, from who got to teach and administrate to how the money would be spent. He'd ban any interference with religious practices. He'd end all race-based teaching and programs, with special emphasis on eradicating anything that smacked of teaching Critical Race Theory.

In a sop to the loud, and angry crowd that vilified anything that even remotely smacked of promoting racial, gender, or LGBT equity, Trump blustered in a campaign video that "I will create a special team to rapidly review every action taken by federal agencies under Biden's 'equity' agenda that will need to be reversed. We will reverse almost all of them."

With a hard-right majority, the SCOTUS in 2024 and beyond was more than willing to knock out anything that even remotely promoted equity and affirmative action. Trump could be as good as his word on this pledge.

Not surprisingly, Trump would again try to do something about his signature pet peeve. That was former President Obama's landmark Affordable Health Care Act. Trump waged what seemed at times during his first term a one-man vendetta against the Act. Again, he was blunt, saying that "Getting much better healthcare than Obamacare for the American people will be a priority of the Trump Administration."

The better way to provide quality healthcare in his view presumably was to make prescription drugs more accessible and affordable, which he claimed he'd do. Biden and then Harris promised the same thing.

Environmentalists would find an implacable enemy in Trump. He consistently led the pack of climate change deniers during his first term. To prove his disbelief in the threat that global warming posed, he refused to have the U.S. have anything to do with the Paris Accords that aimed to reduce greenhouse gas pollution. He did everything possible to gut the Energy Dept. He waged war on green energy expansion.

He tried to gut every pollution-control rule and regulation on the books. Trump made clear that he'd give the oil and gas industry free rein to exploit public lands to extract oil and gas with no regulatory constraints. As Trump crudely put it, "We're going to 'drill, baby, drill' right away."

*****

Then there was the perennial issue of gun control. The NRA practically lionized Trump for repeatedly stroking, praising, and honoring the organization at every turn during his first term. There was little doubt that the political love affair between him and the NRA would continue to blossom. He made that clear in a talk in April 2023 to the Institute for Legislative Action Leadership Forum: "I will take Biden's executive order directing the federal government to target the firearms industry, and I will rip it up and throw it out on day one."

That was certainly sweet music to the NRA's ear. If Trump had anything to do with it, a congressional comprehensive gun control bill would not have a prayer of ever seeing the legislative light of day.

Trump before, during, and after his White House years took every opportunity to shower accolades on SCOTUS justices like Clarence Thomas. He appointed an endless wave of hard-right conservative justices while in office. He tried mightily to revamp the Justice Department to get rid of those he berated as so-called activist prosecutors who went after police misconduct, corporate abuses, and civil liberties violations.

He loudly declared that if re-elected he'd turn the heat up even higher on the Justice Department. He'd emphasize that the Department solely focus on prosecuting violent criminals. To make sure it did, he declared that he "would not hesitate to send in federal law enforcement to restore peace and public safety." Trump would hand the police full unhampered, uninhibited authority, free of any constitutional and civil rights and liberties constraints. They could take any action they deemed necessary to curb crime, including the use of stop and frisk.

Trump had one more powerful weapon in his political arsenal to try to make good on his threat of a total overhaul of the DOJ. When the SCOTUS in a June 2024 decision granted him near full immunity from prosecutions for "official" acts, that came close to a free license to shield his actions done as President, no matter how illicit, from prosecution by the DOJ. If that held, the department would be nothing more than a rubber stamp for Trump.

*****

In polls and surveys in the months before the 2024 election, Trump and the GOP consistently had one clear advantage over Biden and Harris and the Democrats. That was on the handling of the economy. A majority of Americans said they thought Trump handled economic issues better than the Democrats.

Trump took that affirmation and ran with it. He repeatedly boasted he'd again do more to keep American industry in America, boost job creation, cut taxes, and tamp down inflation. In Trump's parlance, he'd be the number one booster of an America First policy on jobs and trade. This supposedly would radically reduce reliance on Chinese imported goods, clamp massive tariffs on foreign-made goods, and stop China and other countries cold from grabbing bigger shares of America's financial and corporate structure.

The global economic and financial institutions were tightly interstitched. The notion of protectionism was quaint, outdated, and unworkable. Trump's America First pitch then was mostly feel-good stuff that revved up crowds and stoked the deep-rooted nativism in wide swatches of Americans. It had little to do with economic and financial reality.

*****

In the same vein, In February 2024 Trump drew the fury of many of the U.S.'s European allies, countless U.S. foreign policy experts and officials, and the Biden administration when he loudly declared that he'd pull the plug on the long-standing U.S. alliance with NATO. The furor over that threat became further inflamed when he declared that as far as he was concerned, Russia could do "whatever the hell they want" in Europe.

Trump was angered at NATO for the member nations supposed refusal to pony up their share of the costs for maintaining the alliance and letting the U.S. front the entire bill. "NATO was busted until I came along," Trump said. "I said, 'Everybody's gonna pay.' They said, 'Well, if we don't pay, are you still going to protect us?' I said, 'Absolutely not.' They couldn't believe the answer."

Trump would almost certainly continue to saber-rattle NATO, presumably on the cost issue during a second term. However, there was little likelihood that the U.S.-NATO alliance would fracture, let alone crumble with a U.S. exit. The threat to Europe of Russian expansionism loomed too large for the U.S. to slacken its support of NATO.

More realistically, Trump would continue to trumpet his supposed clean record for keeping the U.S. out of wars during his first tenure in the Oval Office. This was more Trump mythmaking. Several conflicts raged during his term that the U.S. was either directly or indirectly involved in. Still, as the self-proclaimed peacemaker, he boasted that he'd quickly settle the Ukraine-Russia and Israel-Hamas conflicts in a matter of days. Trump, in contrast to Biden, reduced foreign policy from the complex art of diplomatic negotiation, cooperation, and alignment, to one man's magnetism.

No matter whether it was a domestic or foreign policy issue, Trump sought to ride back into office as the classic man on the white horse with all the answers.

It appeared for a moment that Trump might coast back into office. There was Biden's calamitous performance in their first debate in June 2024, the calls for him to step down from a chorus of Democrats, and his back-and-forth downward numbers in some polls in the immediate aftermath. Added to that was the assassination attempt on Trump in July 2024.

Biden, however, eventually stepped down and now Trump had to face Harris. She brought a new face, new energy, and a new threat to Trump's entire remake of America. Most polls continued to show the race tight. The one sure thing that could be said with certainty about the 2024 presidential campaign was that it was unlike any in modern American presidential election history. Trump made sure of that.

Sources

Introduction

Marina Pitofsky, "Donald Trump repeats comment he
would be a dictator 'for one day' if reelected
in 2024," *USA Today*, 12/11/23, https://
www.usatoday.com/story/news/politics/
elections/2023/12/11/donald-trump-dictator-one-
day-reelected/71880010007/.

1 Send Them All Back

"Trump administration had 'most secure border' in
US history, former president claims," *Sky
News.com*, 1/23/24, https://www.skynews.
com.au/world-news/united-states/trump-
administration-had-most-secure-border-in-
us-history-former-president-claims/video/
b9aca26ccdaafcdd39b096bf54437dbe.

Rachel Siegal, "Trump's Immigration Plan could deal
a major blow to the Job Market," *Washington
Post*, 5/20/24, https://www.washingtonpost.
com/business/2024/05/20/trump-immigration-
undocumented-economy/.

Brooke Singman," Trump says he will carry out the largest
deportation in American history, if elected,"
Fox News, 9/20/23, https://www.foxnews.com/
politics/trump-says-he-will-carry-out-the-largest-
domestic-deportation-operation-in-american-
history-if-elected.

Meg Wagner, "State of the Union 2020," *CNN*, 2/5/20, https://www.cnn.com/politics/live-news/state-of-the-union-2020#h_e8e6ef80d3a0aaf508cf3f8d8ebfbce5.

Tol Kopan, "Key Points in Trump's Immigration Executive orders, *CNN*, 5/19/24, https://www.cnn.com/2017/01/25/politics/donald-trump-immigration-executive-orders/index.html.

Phil Mattingly, "How Trump's First Term May have laid the groundwork to make his radical immigration agenda a reality," *CNN*, 5/19/24, https://www.cnn.com/2024/05/19/politics/donald-trump-immigration-agenda/index.html.

2 "I Am the Law-and-Order President"

Olivia B, Waman, "Trump Declared Himself the 'President of Law and Order.' Here's What People Get Wrong About the Origins of That Idea," *Time*, 6/2/20, https://www.yahoo.com/news/trump-declared-himself-president-law-162728286.html?fr=sycsrp_catchall.

Thompson Reuters, "Trump opposes major police reforms, promises better training," *cbc.ca.*, 6/11/20, https://www.cbc.ca/news/world/trump-police-racist-1.5608678.

Joshua Zitzer, "Donald Trump congratulates Kyle Rittenhouse on his acquittal: 'If that's not self-defense, nothing is," *Business Insider*, 11/20/21, https://www.businessinsider.com/donald-trump-

congratulates-kyle-rittenhouse-on-acquittal-
statement-2021-11.

Peter Grier, "From Goldwater to Trump, The Long History
of Law and Order Politics," *CSM*, 11/2/20, https://
www.csmonitor.com/USA/Politics/2020/0902/
From-Goldwater-to-Trump-the-long-history-of-
Law-and-Order-politics.

Kinsey Crowley, "'A stunning turnabout': Voters and
lawmakers across US move to reverse criminal
justice reform," *USA Today*, 3/11/24, https://www.
usatoday.com/story/news/nation/2024/03/10/
tough-on-crime-policy-resurgence/72868353007/.

German Lopez, "Trump's Criminal Justice Policy,
Explained," *Vox*, 9/11/20, https://www.vox.
com/2020-presidential-election/21418911/donald-
trump-crime-criminal-justice-policy-record.

3 Taking Back the Schools

Kate Sullivan, "Trump Wants to Close the Department of
Education, Joining Calls by GOP Rivals," *CNN*,
9/13/23, https://www.cnn.com/2023/09/13/
politics/trump-department-of-education-
states-2024/index.html.

Rob Schofield, "The Trump Teams radical Plan to gut
American public education, " *Yahoo News*,
5/14/24, https://www.yahoo.com/news/
trump-team-radical-plan-gut-100049515.
html?fr=sycsrp_catchall.

Matthew Stone, "What Would Happen to K-12 in a 2nd Trump Term? A Detailed Policy Agenda Offers Clues," *EdW*, 3/25/24, https://www.edweek.org/policy-politics/what-would-happen-to-k-12-in-a-2nd-trump-term-a-detailed-policy-agenda-offers-clues/2024/03.

4 Impounding the Government

"Impoundment of Appropriated Funds," n.d., https://en.wikipedia.org/wiki/Impoundment_of_appropriated_funds.

Brent D. Griffiths, "Trump was accused of breaking a Nixon-era law by withholding funds to Ukraine. Now, he wants to get rid of it entirely," *Business Insider*, 6/27/23, https://www.businessinsider.com/trump-impoundment-nixon-campaign-pledged-spending-cba-2024-2023.

Anthony Zurcher, "What a Donald Trump second term would look like," *bbc.com*, 11/3/23, https://www.bbc.com/news/world-us-canada-67272569.

Andrew Restuccia, "Why Trump's Drastic Plan to Slash the Government could succeed," *WSJ*, 21/10/23, https://www.msn.com/en-us/news/politics/why-trump-s-drastic-plan-to-slash-the-government-could-succeed/ar-AA1j4FJg.

Paul M. Krawzak, "Trump says he will restore presidential impoundment authority," *rollcall.com*, 6/20/23, https://rollcall.com/2023/06/20/trump-says-hell-restore-presidential-impoundment-authority/.

5 The Diversity Assault

Jessica Guynn, "DEI destroyer in chief? Trump vows to crush 'anti-white' racism if he wins 2024 election," *USA Today*, 5/1/24, https://www.usatoday.com/story/money/2024/05/01/donald-trump-anti-white-racism-dei/73528246007/.

Nicquel Terry Ellis, "DEI efforts are under siege. Here's what experts say is at stake," *CNN*, 1/7/24, https://www.cnn.com/2024/01/07/us/dei-attacks-experts-warn-of-consequences-reaj/index.html.

Jessica Guynn, "Trump tried to crush the 'DEI revolution.' Here's how he might finish the job," *USA Today*, n.d., https://www.msn.com/en-us/news/politics/trump-tried-to-crush-the-dei-revolution-heres-how-he-might-finish-the-job/ar-BB1jg3gz.

"Trump Make America Great Again," https://www.donaldjtrump.com/agenda47.

6 Nine Alitos on the SCOTUS?

Gabby Orr, "Trump praises Supreme Court ruling, calling it 'the biggest win for life in a generation'" *CNN*, 6/25/22, https://www.cnn.com/politics/live-news/roe-wade-abortion-supreme-court-ruling/h_5735252b4da1298eb4f5b302f7c8241d.

Jack Shafer, "Opinion: The Supreme Court is political and always has been," *Politico*, 1/28/22, https://www.politico.com/news/magazine/2022/01/28/supreme-court-is-political-always-has-been-00003224.

Zachary B. Wolf, "Who is Trump's favorite Supreme Court justice? Probably not one of the 3 he nominated," *CNN*, 5/29/24, https://www.cnn.com/2024/05/29/politics/supreme-court-trump-what-matters/index.html.

Isaac Chotiner, "How Trump Transformed the Supreme Court," *New Yorker*, 11/11/21, https://www.newyorker.com/news/q-and-a/how-trump-transformed-the-supreme-court.

Isaac Chotiner, "Donald Trump's Plan to make the presidency more like a kingship," *New Yorker*, 7/18/23, https://www.newyorker.com/news/q-and-a/donald-trumps-plan-to-make-the-presidency-more-like-a-kingship.

Adam Rawnsley, "Team Trump Is Ready to Lose the Supreme Court Immunity Case. They're Celebrating," *Rolling Stone*, 4/24/24, https://www.rollingstone.com/politics/politics-features/trump-celebrating-supreme-court-immunity-heist-1235009838/.

Lawrence Hurley, "How Trump could win at the Supreme Court even if his broad immunity argument was rejected," *NBC*, 4/21/24, https://www.nbcnews.com/politics/supreme-court/trump-win-supreme-court-immunity-argument-rcna148384.

Isaac Chotiner, "Donald Trump's Plan to Make the Presidency More Like a Kingship," *New Yorker*, 7/18/23, https://www.newyorker.com/news/q-and-a/donald-trumps-plan-to-make-the-presidency-more-like-a-kingship.

7 Drill, Baby, Drill

Kaanita Lyer, "Senate Democrats launch investigation into alleged Trump 'quid pro quo' with oil executives," *CNN*, 5/23/24, https://www.cnn.com/2024/05/23/politics/trump-senate-democrats-oil-investigation/index.html.ccccccc

Laura Davison and Jennifer A Dlouhy, "Donald Trump Is the Oil and Gas Industry's Top Choice for President," *Bloomberg.com*, 2/9/24, https://www.bloomberg.com/news/articles/2024-02-09/trump-got-7-4m-from-energy-sector-donors-making-him-their-2024-pick.

Sara Dorn, "Energy Industry Already Giving Trump Millions—While He Promises Big Cutbacks in Seeking $1 Billion Donation," *Forbes*, 5/10/24, https://www.forbes.com/sites/saradorn/2024/05/10/energy-industry-already-giving-trump-millions-while-he-promises-big-cutbacks-in-seeking-1-billion-donation/?sh=1651c2c46bb3.

Rebecca Rommen, "Trump sought $1 billion from oil execs for his 2024 campaign in a deal worth $110 billion to energy giants, reports say," *Business Insider*, 5/24, https://www.msn.com/en-us/news/politics/trump-sought-1-billion-from-oil-execs-for-his-2024-campaign-in-a-deal-worth-110-billion-to-energy-giants-reports-say/ar-BB1mFHVw.

Michael Copley, "A second Trump term could slow the shift from fossil fuels as climate threats grow, *WFAE*, 6/25/24, https://www.wfae.org/energy-environment/2024-06-25/a-second-trump-term-could-slow-the-shift-from-fossil-fuels-as-climate-threats-grow.

Nadja Popovich, et al., "The Trump Administration Rolled Back More Than 100 Environmental Rules. Here's the Full List," *New York Times*, 1/20/21, https://www.nytimes.com/interactive/2020/climate/trump-environment-rollbacks-list.html.

Ella Nilsen, "Biden's EPA is trying to take a huge bite out of the climate crisis. Can it survive Trump's Supreme Court? *CNN*, 5/22/24, https://www.cnn.com/2024/05/22/climate/supreme-court-epa-biden-trump/index.html.

Oliver Milman, "Donald Trump's Energy Plans "Potentially Disastrous" for the Climate," *Mother Jones*, 2/7/24, https://www.motherjones.com/politics/2024/02/donald-trump-epa-energy-climate-policies-fossil-fuel-drill-baby-drill/.

"Agenda47: America Must Have the #1 Lowest Cost Energy and Electricity on Earth," 9/7/23, https://www.donaldjtrump.com/agenda47/agenda47-america-must-have-the-1-lowest-cost-energy-and-electricity-on-earth.

8 Peace Through Strength

Jack Izzo, "Fact Check: Is Trump the Only US President in the Last 72 Years Without A War? *Snopes*, n.d., https://www.msn.com/en-us/news/politics/fact-check-is-trump-the-only-us-president-in-the-last-72-years-without-a-war/ar-AA1n3M3p.

Christopher Giles, "US election 2020: Has Trump kept his promises on the military, *BBC*, 10/16/20, https://www.bbc.com/news/election-us-2020-54060026.

Sam Cabral, "Biden administration blames chaotic Afghan pull-out on Trump," *BBC*, 4/6/23, https://www.bbc.com/news/world-us-canada-65208663.

Tom Bowman, "Trump and the Military: What An Erratic Commander In Chief Leaves Behind, *NPR*, 1/4/21, https://www.npr.org/2021/01/04/951203109/trump-and-the-military-what-an-erratic-commander-in-chief-leaves-behind.

"Agenda47: Rebuilding America's Depleted Military," 7/18/23, https://www.donaldjtrump.com/agenda47/agenda47-rebuilding-americas-depleted-military.

9 Anything Goes—Deregulating America

Douglas Gillison, "If Trump wins, he plans to free Wall Street from 'burdensome regulations,'" *Reuters*, 4/12/24, https://www.reuters.com/markets/us/if-trump-wins-he-plans-free-wall-street-burdensome-regulations-2024-04-12/.

"Agenda47: Liberating America from Biden's Regulatory Onslaught," 4/16/23, https://www.donaldjtrump.com/agenda47/agenda47-liberating-america-from-bidens-regulatory-onslaught.

Zoe Stern, "Trump's Deregulatory Failures," *The Regulatory Review*, 1/31/24, https://www.

theregreview.org/2024/01/31/stern-trumps-deregulatory-failures.

Phillip A. Wallach, Examining some of Trump's deregulation efforts," *Brookings*, 3/8/22, https://www.brookings.edu/articles/examining-some-of-trumps-deregulation-efforts-lessons-from-the-brookings-regulatory-tracker/.

10 "The Greatest Economy in History"

"Agenda47: Joe Biden Has Been a Disaster for the Economy," 3/17/23, https://www.donaldjtrump.com/agenda47/agenda47-joe-biden-has-been-a-disaster-for-the-economy.

Louis Jacobson, "In case you forgot. Two years ago today, we were experiencing the greatest economy in the history of the world," *Politifact*, 10/8/21, https://www.politifact.com/factchecks/2021/oct/08/facebook-posts/no-donald-trump-didnt-lead-greatest-economy-histor/.

Don Lee, "Trump vs. Obama Who has the better record on the economy," *Los Angeles Times*, 10/27/20, https://www.latimes.com/politics/story/2020-10-27/trump-vs-obama-who-really-did-better-on-the-economy.

Dante Chinni, "The Myth of the Trump Economy," *NBC*, 8/23/20, https://www.yahoo.com/news/myth-trump-economy-121817487.html?fr=sycsrp_catchall.

11 Attacking the Sacred Cows: Medicare and Social Security

"Social Security Remains Biggest Thorn in Reagan's Side," *The Oklahoman*, 11/8/81, https://www.oklahoman.com/story/news/1981/11/08/social-security-remains-biggest-thorn-in-reagans-side/60362777007/.

David Rosenbaum, "First Major Cuts in Social Security Proposed in Detailed Reagan Plan," *New York Times*, 5/13/81, https://www.nytimes.com/1981/05/13/us/first-major-cuts-in-social-security-proposed-in-detailed-reagan-plan.html.

Paul Krugman, "Opinion: GOP's war against Medicare and Social Security has been long," *Houston Chronicle*, 2/15/23, https://www.houstonchronicle.com/opinion/outlook/article/paul-krugman-medicare-social-security-gop-biden-17784328.php.

Tara Golshan, "Trump said he wouldn't cut Medicaid, Social Security, and Medicare. His 2020 budget cuts all 3," *Vox*, 3/12/19, https://www.vox.com/policy-and-politics/2019/3/12/18260271/trump-medicaid-social-security-medicare-budget-cuts.

Brett Samuels, "Trump cleans up remarks about 'cutting' Social Security and Medicare," *Yahoo News*, 3/14/24, https://www.yahoo.com/news/trump-cleans-remarks-cutting-social-131455108.html?fr=sycsrp_catchall.

Kate Sullivan, "Trump suggests he's open to cuts to Medicare and Social Security after attacking primary rivals over the issue," *CNN*, 3/11/24, https://www.cnn.com/2024/03/11/politics/trump-entitlements-social-security-medicare/index.html.

12 Trump's War on Drugs

Danny Cevallos, "Trump wants the death penalty for drug traffickers. He's got it," *NBC*, 3/20/18, https://www.nbcnews.com/politics/donald-trump/trump-wants-death-penalty-drug-traffickers-he-s-got-it-n858201.

Dina Fine Maron, "Is Trump's Opioid Strategy a 'War on Drugs' Relapse?" *SCIAM*, 3/2018, https://www.scientificamerican.com/article/is-trumps-opioid-strategy-a-war-on-drugs-relapse/.

"Issues," donaldjtrump.com, accessed 1/6/23, https://www.donaldjtrump.com/issues.

Centers for Disease Control and Prevention, "Drug Overdose Deaths in the United States, 2001–2021," 12/2022, https://www.cdc.gov/nchs/products/databriefs/db457.htm#fig4.

"As president, Donald Trump 'marshaled the full power of government to stop deadly drugs, opioids, and fentanyl from coming into our country. As a result, drug overdose deaths declined nationwide for the first time in nearly 30 years,'" *Politifact*, https://www.politifact.com/factchecks/2023/jan/09/donald-trump/fact-checking-donald-trump-drug-overdose-rates-his/.

13 Trump's China Syndrome

Matt Egan, Trump's new trade war would cost middle-class families at least $1,700 a year, report warns, *CNN*, 5/21/24, https://www.cnn.com/2024/05/21/business/trump-trade-war-tariffs-china/index.html.

Ryan Haas, "More Pain than GAIN-How the Trade War Hurt America," *Brookings*, 8/7/20, https://www.brookings.edu/articles/more-pain-than-gain-how-the-us-china-trade-war-hurt-america/.

Filip Demott, "Trump's wide-reaching tariff plan will hurt average Americans and only help the top 1%, Nobel-winning economist says," *Markets Insider*, n.d., https://www.msn.com/en-us/money/markets/trump-s-wide-reaching-tariff-plan-will-hurt-average-americans-and-only-help-the-top-1-nobel-winning-economist-says/ar-BB1pm8JP.

Jonathan Chait, "Trump Advisor Admits He Lost Trade War. He's Going to Lose the Next One Too," *New York Magazine*, 6/18/24, https://nymag.com/intelligencer/article/trump-china-tariff-adviser-admits-trade-deal-failed.html.

Christine Pazzanese, "Researcher details findings on policy that failed to boost U.S. employment even as it scored political points," *Harvard Gazette*, 3/13/24, https://news.harvard.edu/gazette/story/2024/03/larger-lesson-about-tariffs-in-a-move-that-helped-trump-but-not-the-country/.

Pew Research Center, "War & International Conflict," https://www.pewresearch.org/topic/international-affairs/international-issues/war-international-conflict-2/.

14 Boys Must Be Boys, Girls Must Be Girls

Colllin Binley, "Judge blocks Biden's Title IX rule in four states, dealing a blow to protections for LGBTQ+ students," *apnews.com*, 6/13/24, https://apnews.com/article/title-ix-transgender-sports-campus-sexual-assault-77f524b4ed8fcc2aecd5e863b0442bf4.

Orio Rummler, "A second Trump term would double down on erasing transgender rights. Here's how advocates are preparing," *Yahoo News*, 6/16/24, https://www.yahoo.com/news/second-trump-term-double-down-092136489.html.

Erica L. Green, et.al., "'Transgender' Could Be Defined Out of Existence Under Trump Administration," *New York Times*, 10/21/18, https://www.nytimes.com/2018/10/21/us/politics/transgender-trump-administration-sex-definition.html.

15 "Black Jobs"

Rob Wile, "Black Jobs? Trump Draws pushback after anti-immigration rant," *NBC*, 6/28/24, https://www.nbcnews.com/news/nbcblk/trumps-anti-immigration-black-jobs-reactions-presidential-debate-rcna159375.

Fabiola Cineas, "No, Trump hasn't been the best president for Black America since Lincoln," *Vox*, 10/21/20, https://www.vox.com/21524499/what-trump-has-done-for-black-people.

Amand Terkel, "Trump says the Black People like him because he's been discriminated against in the legal system," *NBC*, 2/23/24, https://www.nbcnews.com/politics/donald-trump/trump-black-people-discriminated-legal-system-rcna140305.

Earl Ofari Hutchinson, "Why Trump Claims so Many Black People Love Him," *Thehutchinsonreport.com*, 3/3/24, http://www.thehutchinsonreport.net/why-trump-claims-so-many-blacks-love-him/.

16 Smashing the Deep State

Bob Ortega, et al., "What Trump's war on the 'Deep State' could mean: 'An army of suck-ups,'" *CNN*, 4/27/24, https://www.cnn.com/2024/04/27/politics/trump-federal-workers-2nd-term-invs/index.html.

Donald P. Moniyhan," Trump Has a Plan for Destroying the Deep State," *New York Times*, 11/27/23, https://www.nytimes.com/2023/11/27/opinion/trump-deep-state-schedule-f.html.

Russell Berman, "The Open Plot to Dismantle the Federal Government," *The Atlantic*, 9/23/23, https://www.theatlantic.com/politics/archive/2023/09/trump-desantis-republicans-dismantle-deep-state/675378/.

Franco Ordonez, "Trump allies craft plans to give him
unprecedented power if he wins the White
House," *NPR*, 12/6/23, https://www.npr.
org/2023/12/06/1217562544/trump-and-insiders-
craft-plans-for-unprecedented-power.

Aisla Slisco, "Trump to 'Dismantle Deep State' with 'Truth
and Reconciliation Commission,'" *Newsweek*,
3/21/23, https://www.newsweek.com/trump-
dismantle-deep-state-truth-reconciliation-
commission-1789374.

17 Remaking America—*PROJECT 2025*

Steve Contorno, "Trump claims not to know who is behind
Project 2025. A CNN review found at least 140
people who worked for him are involved," *CNN*,
7/11/24, https://www.cnn.com/2024/07/11/
politics/trump-allies-project-2025/index.html.

ABC News, "Trump is trying to distance himself from
Project 2025," *ABC*, n.d., https://www.msn.com/
en-us/news/politics/trump-is-trying-to-distance-
himself-from-project-2025/ar-BB1pENP6.

Rachel Barber, 'What is Project 2025? Right-wing plan
to attack abortion access, Obamacare, LGBTQ+
rights," *USA Today*, 7/11/24, https://www.usatoday.
com/story/news/2024/07/11/what-is-project-2025-
is-oklahoma-connected-to-it/74353845007/.

Mike Wendling, "Project 2025: A wish list for a Trump
presidency, explained," *BBC*, 7/12/24, https://www.
bbc.com/news/articles/c977njnvq2do.

Heritage Foundation, Project 2025, 1/31/23, https://
www.heritage.org/conservatism/commentary/
project-2025.

Heritage Foundation, *Mandate for Leadership:
The Conservative Promise*, 2023,
https://static.project2025.org/2025_
MandateForLeadership_FULL.pdf.

18 "This is Not a Gun Problem"

Jonathan Allen, "Trump says mass shootings are not
'a gun problem' as 2024 GOP hopefuls pledge
loyalty to the NRA," *NBC*, 4/14/23, https://www.
nbcnews.com/politics/donald-trump/trump-
says-mass-shootings-arent-gun-problem-nra-
convention-rcna79775.

Nathan Layne, "Trump vows to undo Biden gun
restrictions if re-elected," *Reuters*, 2/10/24,
https://www.reuters.com/world/us/trump-
vows-undo-biden-gun-restrictions-if-re-
elected-2024-02-10/.

Conclusion

Kaleda Rahman, "What Mass Deportation Under Trump
Could Look Like," *Newsweek*, 6/26/24, https://
www.newsweek.com/what-mass-deportation-
trump-look-like-1916649.

Jessica Guynn, "Trump tried to crush the 'DEI revolution.'
Here's how he might finish the job, *USA Today*,
3/3/24, https://www.usatoday.com/story/

money/2024/03/03/trump-plans-crush-dei-
affirmative-action/72774345007/.

Phillip A. Wallach, "Examining Some of Trump's
Deregulation Efforts: Lessons from the Brookings
Regulatory Tracker," *Brookings*, 3/8/22, https://
www.brookings.edu/articles/examining-some-of-
trumps-deregulation-efforts-lessons-from-the-
brookings-regulatory-tracker/.

Gram Slattery, et al., "Donald Trump wants to control
the Justice Department and FBI. His allies have a
plan," *Reuters*, 5/29/24, https://www.reuters.com/
world/us/donald-trump-wants-control-justice-
department-fbi-his-allies-have-plan-2024-05-17/.

Robert Hamilton, "Our Allies are Terrified of a President
Trump 2.0 | Opinion," *Newsweek*, n.d., https://
www.msn.com/en-us/news/other/our-allies-
are-terrified-of-a-president-trump-2-0-opinion/
ar-BB1pOThs.

Bibliography

Arnsdorf, Isaac. *Finish What We Started: The MAGA Movement's Ground War to End Democracy* (New York, 2024).

Balog, David. *Trump's "Project 2025" Would End LGBTQ Protections* (Independently Published, 2024).

Bergen Peter. *Trump and His Generals: The Cost of Chaos* (New York, 2019).

Berkshire, Jennifer, et al. *A Wolf at the Schoolhouse Door: The Dismantling of Public Education and the Future of School* (New York, 2023).

Bongino, Dan. *Follow the Money: The Shocking Deep State Connections of the Anti-Trump Cabal* (New York, 2020).

Brooks, Jefferson. *Project 2025 Explained: Understanding the Heritage Foundation's Mandate for Leadership* (Independently Published, 2024).

Burns, Alexander and Martin, Jonathan. *This Will Not Pass: Trump, Biden, and the Battle for America's Future* (New York, 2022).

Cocorinos, Lee. *The Assault on Diversity: An Organized Challenge to Racial and Gender Diversity* (New York, 2003).

Cogan, John F. *The High Cost of Good Intentions: A History of U.S. Federal Entitlement Programs* (Stanford, CA ,2019).

Davis Hirschfeld, Julie, et al. *Border Wars: Inside Trump's Assault on Immigration* (New York, 2019).

Drucker, David. *In Trump's Shadow: The Battle for 2024 and the Future of the GOP* (New York, 2021).

Haberman, Maggie. *Confidence Man: The Making of Donald Trump and the Breaking of America* (New York, 2022).

Hanson, Victor. *The Case for Trump* (New York, 2024).

Kaplan, David A. *The Most Dangerous Branch: Inside the Supreme Court in the Age of Trump* (New York, 2019).

Klein, Naomi. *No is Not Enough: Resisting Trump's Shock Politics and Winning the World We Need* (New York, 2017).

Lacombe, Matthew. *Firepower: How the NRA Turned Gun Owners into a Political Force* (Princeton, NJ, 2021).

Lafer, Arthur and Moore, Stephen. *Trumponomics: Inside the America First Plan to Revive Our Economy* (All Points Books, 2018).

Murray, Melissa and Weismann, Andrew. *The Trump Indictments: The Historic Charging Documents with Commentary* (New York, 2024).

Perry, Luke. *The 2020 Presidential Election: Key Issues and Regional Dynamics* (New York, 2022).

Romney, Richard B. *Project 2025 Meets Agenda 47: Aligning National Priorities and Policies* (Independently Published, 2024).

Stone, Jeremy. *Trump Returns For 2025! The U.S. VS China (Surviving the New World Order)* (Independently Published, 2021).

Winslow, Luke. *American Catastrophe: Fundamentalism, Climate Change, Gun Rights, and the Rhetoric of Donald J. Trump* (Columbus, OH, 2020).

Wurt, William. *Agenda 47: Trump's Vision for America's Future* (Independently Published, 2024).

About the Author

Earl Ofari Hutchinson is the author of multiple books on race and politics in America. He is a political analyst. He has appeared on MSNBC and on CNN. His books include the trilogy on the Obama Years: *The Obama Legacy, How Obama Governed: The Year of Crisis and Challenge*, and *How Obama Won*. His most recent books are *The Trump Challenge to Black America, From King to Obama: Witness to a Turbulent History, Bring Back the Poll Tax—The GOP War on Voting Rights*, and *Is Biden Really Too Old?: The Politics of Age and Ageism in America*.

Index